MAKE MONEY HELPING PEOPLE

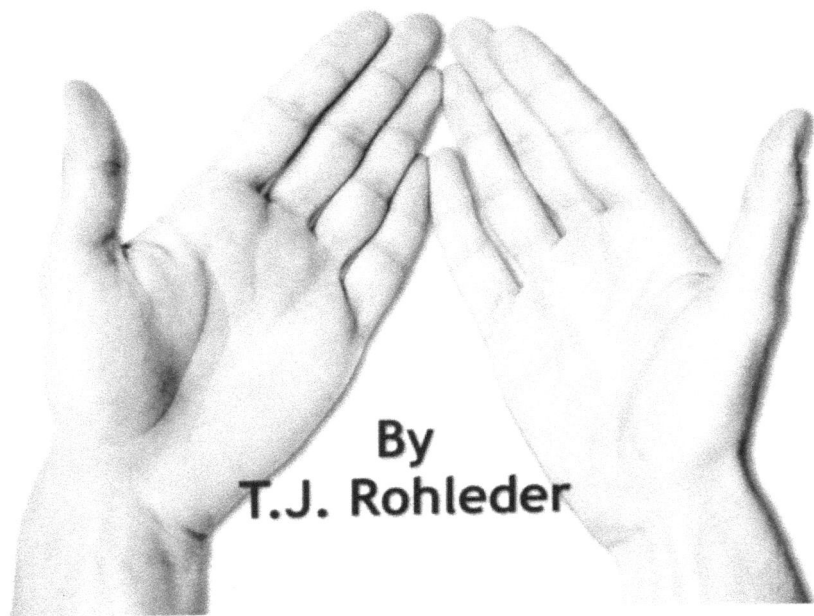

By
T.J. Rohleder

You can have anything
in life you want,
if you'll only help
enough other people
get what they want.

— Zig Ziglar

*Thank you Al Branca for
making all of this possible!*

TABLE OF CONTENTS

FORWARD

By Russ von Hoelscher

A Business in a Book!

I was thrilled when T.J. asked me to write a few words about his new book "Make Money Helping People!" As you'll see, this is not just a book with a bunch of great-sounding ideas in it. It's a complete home business that can make you tremendous sums of money. I love this opportunity and know you will, too. The reason is simple: There has never been such a more effective way to make so much money and do so much good. This opportunity is so good, I'm jumping in on it, too! I believe this is the money-maker that will help many achieve financial freedom.

For over 40 years, I've been helping average people make above average incomes. That's how I met T.J. Rohleder. It was 1989. T.J. and his wife Eileen had just started their first mail order business six months earlier. They had stumbled onto a really great idea and business was booming. Their sales were around $16,000 a month. And because I had over 20 years of experience at that time and because they had a great business model and did what I advised them to do, I was able to help them turn that small amount into millions. Within 9 months, I helped them go from $16,000 a month to as much as $100,000 a week. And I was able to help them turn that into a grand total of over $10,000,000 in their first 5 years.

T.J. tells people that all of the money he's brought in over the years is because of me and the help I gave him. He says it would have never happened if he and Eileen had not met me. I always appreciate hearing that. And I am grateful for the fact that I was there for them when they were first getting started. But they were easy Clients to help, because they had such a great business model to begin with and then did everything I asked them to do. This made it easy for me to help them do what it took to become financially set for life.

Now, T.J. is Offering to Do the Same Thing for You.

I am proud to endorse this book. The second section especially contains some of the ultimate tips, tricks and strategies I first taught T.J. in his early years. Plus, it contains many secrets he discovered from other marketing experts. And to top it off, his new breakthrough (called "The Easy Passive Income System") is built around a revolutionary opportunity that's designed to let you earn enormous sums of passive income by solving huge problems for millions of other people.

This is something I firmly believe can

ultimately generate many millions of dollars for all of us who are involved in it and now you can be one of these lucky people!

How Much Will You Make?

Well, as T.J. will make quite clear; nobody can say for sure how much if any amount of money you'll will make in any business, no matter how amazing it is. However, he will do his best to show you that this opportunity could potentially make you as much as $100,000 a year or more. The best part; this can be pure passive income for you! It's money that will come to you automatically, because of one simple and easy step you do. That may sound hard to believe right now, but read on and let him show you how simple this can work. Because as you're about to discover; the amount of money you can make with this home business [that T.J. reveals in this book] has little or nothing to do with the amount of time and work you do. I'm so excited about this. You will be, too!

Making more money with less time and effort is the ultimate money-making opportunity.

So go over this book carefully. Discover all the secrets. And remember, an opportunity to put in a few minutes of easy and enjoyable work from you kitchen table and then get paid an ongoing passive income only comes along once in a lifetime, but you have one here. You've taken the first step by reading my words. Now turn the page, continue reading. Then follow the simple instructions at the end. Do this and get started right now, while all this is fresh in your mind. You'll be glad you did!

All the best and may God bless.

Russ von Hoelscher,
Hoelscher Marketing Group
El Cajon, California
(619) 588-2155

<u>INTRODUCTION</u>

Thank you for purchasing this book and making the time to go through it. This tells me that you are serious about making money for yourself. And that's exactly what this small book is all about. So let's get right to it.

For starters, did you know there are only 3 ways to make money?

YES, only 3.

Here they are...

METHOD #1:

You Can Sell Your Time for Money.

This is the way 99% of the people make almost all of their money. Everyone from day laborers who slave under the hot sun for minimum wage, to brain surgeons who get paid thousands of dollars an hour. All of these people are selling their time for money.

METHOD #2:

You Can Sell a Product or Service
or Combination of Both.

With this second method, your money comes from the sale of some product or service, not the amount of time you work. This is a much smarter way to make money. In fact, the world is filled with many millionaires who make almost all of their money with this second powerful method.

But the real secret to making money is to use the final method.

Just look...

METHOD #3:

PASSIVE INCOME! You Use Your Money
to Make More Money Automatically.

The second method is quite capable of
making you a lot of money. But the third method
of making money has made more people wealthy
than the other two combined. With this final
method, you are putting your money into income-
producing assets that automatically make you
more money... All you do is sit back and get paid
for things that have very little – or nothing – to do
with the amount of time and work you do.

And now for the best news...

Our Easy Passive Income System that you'll
read about in this book is one of the most
powerful ways to make money, because ALL the

money you can make will come from the 2nd and 3rd methods which are responsible for the GIANT fortunes that are made by the world's richest people.

A.   All of your wealth is generated from the transactions that are made by hundreds or even thousands of our DISCOUNT PRESCRIPTION CARDHOLDERS who use their cards to save up to 87% off on each FDA approved drug. They use our card to save money on their prescription medications and you get paid each and every time a prescription is filled. As you'll see, this can pay you huge profits!

But you will not be offering these free prescription savings cards yourself.

B.   All of the income that you generate

can be made for you by groups of other people. I'll go over all of this in complete detail in the first few chapters. As you'll see, these people do all of the "work" and you get paid passive income for many months and even years! This is so exciting and can be extremely lucrative for you!

When you fully understand how all of this is designed to make you thousands of dollars a month – and add it all together – you'll see why I call our Easy Passive Income System...

"One of the World's Greatest Ways to Become Financially Set for Life."

This gives you the ultimate way to cash-in with the same two methods that the world's richest people use to make their fortune. The amount of money you can earn has very little or even nothing to do with the amount of actual time and work you put in.

And this leads to the biggest benefit of all...

**Because We Can Run
All of This for You –
It is Possible for You to Make
Thousands of Dollars a Month
with No Hard Work!**

Yes, I know how absolutely unbelievable that sounds – and BOLD statements such as this should make you very skeptical... After all, sitting back and getting paid up to thousands of dollars a month does sound way too good to be true.

But this is exactly what our Easy Passive Income System is deigned to do for you.

Of course, there are no promises and

guarantees that you will make one hundred thousand dollars a year or any specific sum of money for doing no hard work – but the potential to get paid many thousands of dollars for letting other people do almost everything for you is definitely here! That's a mighty bold statement. I do not blame you for being skeptical about this. But, by the time you're done with this book, I'll prove it's true.

This is so much better than all of the other low-cost business opportunities that you can get involved in, such as network marketing.

There are a few things I do love about those types of opportunities:

1. I love the idea of "people helping other people."

2. I love any wealth-making method that

lets the average person make money from the efforts of other people. After all, that's what making huge sums of passive income is all about!

3.   I love the fact that those opportunities let you get started for very little money. And the fact that some people go onto making huge six figure incomes.

As for everything else about those kind of opportunities – I hate it all:

A.   I hate all of the personal selling that must be done.

B.   I hate all of the lies and deception about how the average person can easily make thousands of dollars overnight – when in reality it can take years to build a big organization that makes serious money.

Now here is the most exciting thing...

Our Easy Passive Income System gives you all of the greatest benefits of Direct Response Marketing and network marketing – without any of the side effects.

This is designed to let you sit back and make a fortune from the time, work and money of as many as hundreds of other people.

The more you understand this – the more thrilled you will be!

So please read this book carefully. If you are as serious as I believe you are about making money, you will be SHOCKED and AMAZED before you are halfway through!

But for right now, let me tell you a little about me...

OUR RAGS-TO-RICHES STORY

For many years my wife, Eileen, and I struggled for every dollar. We never had enough money to pay all of our bills. Our life was a constant frustration. We were poverty poor. And we had no hope for getting out of our poverty.

√   We had no special education.

√   We were not born into a family that had a lot of money.

√   We had no special skills or knowledge.

√   We had none of the things you need to get rich.

But we did have one thing going for us...

We hated our lives of poverty and we were convinced that there was something better out there for us. We were proud to be Americans and firmly believed in this great country and all of the opportunities that were available to average people like us.

Eileen and I knew that other average people who had less going for them than we had were getting rich! We heard all the rags-to-riches stories of people who had started with very little or even no money and turned it into a huge fortune. And somewhere along the line we started to believe that I was more than possible to make a lot of money. So we took BOLD action on our dreams of getting rich.

Here's what we did:

> We started to send away for every moneymaking program we could find that sounded different and was

inexpensive.

> We joined a bunch of network marketing companies.

> We began listening to motivational audio programs and reading all the success books we could get our hands on.

All this fanned the flames of our desire.

It was Like Throwing a 55-gallon Drum of Jet Fuel Onto a Raging Fire. Now Our Belief That We Could Actually Get Rich Became an Obsession!

I call it my magnificent obsession. And to make a long story short – within less than a handful of years – we were millionaires.

Yes, all of our biggest dreams of making a

fortune came true. In fact, when the riches began coming to us, they came so fast we thought we were dreaming! On more than one occasion we would look at each other and just start laughing uncontrollably! We would literally pinch ourselves to make sure this was really happening.

And it was happening...

In fact, Within 5 Years from the Time
Things Started Turning Around for Us,
We Brought in a Total of Over $10,000,000.

But wait a minute. Please do not think that I'm bragging – because I'm not. We all know people who try to show off and I can't stand being around these people. I'm sure you feel the same way.

No, I'm not bragging about the millions of dollars that came pouring in within a few short years. NO WAY. In fact, the only reason I tell you our rags-to-riches story is to help you realize that the same thing could happen to you!

Yes, it is possible for you to get very rich in a short period of time – just like we did!

In fact, I will be as bold as saying this...

I Firmly Believe That You Could End Up Making Even More Money Than We Made!

All you have to do is discover the perfect opportunity that is designed to make you a lot of money. Just find the right opportunity and get the right help from the right people – and you will have the amazing power to make millions... Just like we did!

I firmly believe that this revolutionary new Easy Passive Income System can be the perfect

opportunity that turns everything around for you –
just like our first discovery made us instant
millionaires! I also believe that many of the people
who get involved with us will make thousands of
dollars a month with the secrets in this book and
YOU can be one of these lucky people!

So thank you for purchasing this book and
making the time to go over it. This was a life-
changing decision for you. That may sound like
hype right now. And I don't blame you for having
some strong doubts. But please go over this
small book carefully and prove to yourself that this
really is the ultimate way to make huge sums of
passive income from the comfort and privacy of
your own home. Then follow the simple
instructions in back and get started today.

SECTION ONE

How to Make Money
and Do So Much Good
for So Many Others.

CHAPTER ONE

How to Get Paid Every Time a Prescription is Filled!

According to The Kaiser Family Foundation, Doctors are writing over four billion prescriptions for drugs in America every year. That's an average of roughly 13 prescriptions for each man, woman, and child... every year! Now we have discovered how YOU can make money by helping people save up to 87% off on each FDA-approved drug at over 54,000 pharmacies nationwide. We're offering to let you partner with us and cash in with our secrets.

This book tells you everything you need

to know.

Our Easy Passive Income System is very simple to understand and easy to use. And as you'll see, this is designed to generate huge sums of passive income for you.

It's as simple as A-B-C:

A.   You'll be using our easy hands-off method to help groups raise money by giving away our free valuable Discount Prescription Card.

B.   Our free card saves people up to 87% off on each FDA approved drug at 54,000 pharmacies nationwide.

C.   You get paid every time a cardholder fills their prescriptions!

Read on to get all of the exciting and

profitable facts!

You'll see that:

* You can make money and help a lot of other people.

* You can make big money in as little as 10-minutes a day.

* You can get paid a pure passive income... for life!

* You could potentially get paid up to $875 to as much as $5,250 a month or more, for letting our system help the groups who need to raise money.

* Other people will do most of the work for you...

* You make money with:

NO long hours. NO personal selling.
NO hard work. NO experience.
NO large start-up cost. NO inventory.
NO headaches. NO hassles!

Here are the Facts:

In spite of advances in medicine and technology, the cost of prescription drug prices continue to soar to record heights. Deductibles have risen as insurance companies try to keep their costs down under the Affordable Care Act. Millions of Americans are rightly concerned about their ability to continue to afford the prescription drugs they need to survive and live healthy lives.

But now, our free prescription drug savings card (The Bethesda Discount Prescription Card) gives everyone access to THE LOWEST PRICES on the prescription drugs they need. In fact, consumers who own our discount prescription cards have already saved a whopping $179,109,815 off the regular prices of the prescription drugs they need. That's almost $180 million dollars – and the savings increases every single day!

Savings of between 25% to 75% and even 87% are common. In some cases, our cardholders have saved up to 98.12%. That sounds unbelievable, but here's a few recent real-life "extreme savings" examples:

Drug Type	Retail Price	Member Paid	Savings	Pharmacy
Ondansestron	$959.65	$17.99	98.12%	Cleveland Clinic
Famotidine	$150.32	$10.98	92.69%	New Care
Sotalol	$530.46	$27.83	94.75%	Kmart
Hydrocortisone	$212.99	$11.53	94.58%	Target
Clobetasol	$222.35	$16.80	92.44%	Kroger

These extreme savings of up to 98.12% off retail are amazing, but true! Oftentimes, the savings are lower, and sometimes your insurance might offer you the best savings. But so far, our members have saved over $179 million dollars using our card.

There is a huge and growing need to save up to 87% on all prescription medications – and we have discovered an easy way that YOU can cash-in from the huge demand.

Americans pay some of the highest retail costs for prescription drugs in the world. And even for those who have insurance, the deductibles and co-pays put even necessary drugs out of reach for many families, forcing them to choose between medicine or food. For these families on the fringe, the ability to have one more option that can save them money is a lifesaver.

If the card is free, how do you make money?

Through a partnership with a major national health technology company, our absolutely free DISCOUNT PRESCRIPTION CARD helps people save money by solving the terrible problem of runaway drug costs.

Here's the secret: Each time a prescription is filled at a pharmacy, profit is made on the sale of the drug. That's just common sense. Everybody knows that. But what you may not realize is that a lot of different people make money on that drug, the drug manufacturer, the local pharmacy, the insurance provider, and/or the DISCOUNT PRESCRIPTION CARD provider. LOTS OF PEOPLE GET PAID each time a prescription is filled.

Now You Can Be One of Them.

Our core system allows Affiliates to make passive cash by using our easy methods to get our discount drug cards into the hands of people who desperately need to save money on their prescription costs. As an affiliate, you can get paid a passive residual income on every prescription filled, when our card was used to get the discount. Plus, you continue to make money as families go back to the pharmacy for refills and new prescriptions. In fact, once our card is used, it usually stays in the pharmacy's records system, so you can continue to get credit for prescriptions each time they are filled and refilled, month after month.

BUT WAIT... That's only the beginning of how you can make money.

Because Our Easy Passive Income System Lets You Make Even More Money by Tapping into a Massive Source of People Who are Eager to Do All of the Work for You to Get These Discount Cards into the Hands of Hundreds or Thousands of Others... Even Faster.

In fact, as you'll see, this system has the

potential to pay you up to $875 to $5,250 a month or more in passive income. And you can do everything in as little as 10 minutes a day. It's easy and fun! This book reveals all the exciting details.

I realize that getting paid up to thousands of dollars a month in passive income by putting in a few minutes of easy, enjoyable work from your kitchen table might sound hard to believe. But by the time you're finished going through this book, you'll have all the secrets. And you can quickly get started by following the simple instructions in the last chapter.

THE SECRET:

Okay, this is where it starts to get exciting. Earlier, I told you that our Easy Passive Income System lets you make money by tapping into a secret source of people who are eager to help you pass out our DISCOUNT PRESCRIPTION CARDS.

Are you ready to hear who this secret group of people is? Okay, here we go...

Our system is designed to let you make huge sums of money by helping non-profit groups raise the funds they need, while paying you an automatic residual income on all the "work" they do.

As you'll see, this can give you complete financial security for life, while helping to do SO MUCH GOOD for so many others. And isn't that what it's all supposed to be about? YES!!!

As I will prove to you...

There Has NEVER Been a Way to Make Up to Thousands of Dollars a Month, While Also Helping So Many Others at the Same Time... Until Now!

There are 3 basic components of our Passive Income Fundraising Program:

1. Helping groups raise huge sums of money without the headaches and hassles most fundraisers require...

2. Helping people save money on their prescription medications...

3. And paying YOU huge sums of passive income!

The More You Know About This Amazing Way to Stay Home and Get Paid a Passive Income for Life – the More Excited You Will Be!

So read on. If you like to make money while helping others, you're going to love this!

<u>CHAPTER TWO</u>

The Four Problems
We Solve.

As with all honest and legitimate home-based business opportunities – if you want to make the MAXIMUM amount of money in the minimum time – you must SOLVE SOME MAJOR PROBLEMS for as many people as possible.

There is no other way to become financially independent.

Just find millions of people with HUGE PROBLEMS and then discover or develop a product or service that solves these problems in the BIGGEST WAY... If you can solve a big enough problem for enough people, then you can make a lot of money and enjoy complete and total FINANCIAL SECURITY.

This is what you can have when you get involved in this proven program.

Now let me tell you how our Easy Passive Income System solves four MAJOR PROBLEMS for many people, including you...

PROBLEM #1:

Millions of people are paying too much for their prescription drugs. Americans pay the highest cost for prescription drugs in the world. And insurance deductibles and co-pay costs are soaring. The discounts we help them get are sorely needed throughout the USA as many people have to decide to buy medicine over food. Our absolutely free DISCOUNT PRESCRIPTION CARD is an exciting way to help people save money by solving this terrible problem. After all, who wouldn't accept a free card that let them save money on something (medicine) that they have to buy anyhow?!

PROBLEM #2:

Thousands of groups desperately need to raise money for all of their group activities. These groups depend on supporters to give them the money they need. And yet, many of the group members HATE all of the things they have to constantly do to raise money. This is NOT the reason they joined the group and yet, they're FORCED to do it. What's more, this fundraising must constantly be done. IT NEVER ENDS. This month, they're selling candy bars, next month it's Christmas wrapping paper, and then the following month it might be some kind of raffle tickets to a charity event. Many of the group members HATE DOING THIS, and yet they must do it to be part of the group and to raise money for all of the activities the group is involved in.

PROBLEM #3:

The friends and family of these group members hate the fact that they are CONSTANTLY being hit up for money for stupid stuff they'd never buy otherwise. Most people love to give, but hate the fact that they are constantly being asked to give more money... They have what fundraising industry insiders call DONOR BURNOUT. The people who care the most and give the most money are constantly being pressured to give more and more and more money. They begin to feel manipulated and taken advantage of because they are treated like an ATM Machine...

PROBLEM #4:

Many people like you need a way to make more money, without all of the headaches and hassles of selling. There is no shortage of home-based business opportunities. Each one 'claims' they can help you make all the money you want and need. And yet, most of these opportunities are loaded with too many problems. And most of them require you to be a master salesperson or talk with prospective customers all day long.

Some are worthless schemes that will cost you money but never make you one red cent.

Our program is different, we've made it a rewarding experience for you, because...

This Passive Income System Solves ALL FOUR Problems and Gives You the Potential Power to Make a Passive Income While Also Doing SO MUCH GOOD for SO MANY OTHERS.

SOLUTION #1:

Our DISCOUNT PRESCRIPTION CARD helps people save up to 87% off on each FDA approved drug at 54,000 pharmacies nationwide.

SOLUTION #2:

This lets thousands of different groups raise the money they want and need without having to beg friends, family, and neighbors to buy something they don't even want! Now these groups can do JUST ONE simple and easy fundraising program (by passing out an unlimited number of our free colorful DISCOUNT PRESCRIPTION CARDS or sending emails to people they know) and passively raise money that keeps coming in for many months and even years.

SOLUTION #3:

The friends and family members feel no

pressure. The group members simply pass out the free cards to friends, family, and supporters of the group or get them to go to our website and instantly download their complementary DISCOUNT PRESCRIPTION CARD. This helps the cardholder get the absolute lowest prices on the prescriptions they need at over 54,000 pharmacies throughout the United States.

Everyone wins! The groups win, because they earn a passive income from a simple-to-use fundraising program that beats all the others, hands-down. Their group can get a very nice check every single month, even if each group member passes out a small number of these cards. And their supporters win, because they get an easy way to help the group raise money that doesn't cost them anything. In fact, it saves them money!

SOLUTION #4:

But you are the biggest winner! Because, as

an Affiliate of our Easy Passive Income System, you will use our complete system that lets you make money in as little as 10 minutes a day. You'll do everything from the comfort and privacy of your own home. This gives you a complete way to get paid a passive monthly income in just minutes a day. Please study the mathematical examples in Chapter Four to see how much money you could potentially make when various numbers of groups pass out our DISCOUNT PRESCRIPTION CARDS. As you'll see, this has the power to make you a huge passive income!

As you'll see – for only a very small start-up fee – you now have the potential power to make hundreds or even thousands of dollars a month, for using our 20-second processing system that's designed to introduce our unique Program to the non-profit groups.

You do one simple step. We do the rest.

This step is based on the methods that have brought us millions of dollars... All the secrets can be yours when you get involved in our Easy Passive Income System.

Get started today and I promise:

1. You can get started now for a very low fee. Then you can do it all from your kitchen table, in as little as a few minutes a day. It's simple and easy. Just use our copyrighted 20-second processing system that introduces our program to the non-profit groups who need more money.

2. It only takes an average of 20 seconds to process our mail for each non-profit group.

3. This 20-second system is so simple a 10-year old child could do it.

4.   This simple but vital step introduces our Program to the groups who need to RAISE MONEY for their group activities.

5.   We work with the group leaders to help them raise all the money their group needs, by simply getting our DISCOUNT PRESCRIPTION CARDS into the hands of their friends and family members.

6.   The 20-second mail processing system is your only requirement. This one very small, but extremely vital step can be done right from your kitchen table.

7.   You'll get paid for all of the prescriptions, each time they're filled and re-filled.

Just sit back... process each piece of our mail... and let our proven marketing system introduce our Passive Income Fundraising Program to the groups.

Each piece of mail takes about 20 seconds to process per group.

It's very simple and easy.

We do everything else.

And you get paid every time a prescription gets filled.

We'll work closely with the groups to help them raise all the money they want. We'll make it easy for them to get our DISCOUNT PRESCRIPTION CARD into the hands of as many of their supporters as possible. This lets them save up to 87% OFF on each FDA approved drug at 54,000 pharmacies nationwide and help the group raise all the money they want and need.

It's a win/win/win situation:

√   The group wins, because they get an easy and automatic way to raise all of the money they need for all of their group activities.

√   Their supporters win, because the friends and family members (and the group members themselves) save a lot of money on all of their prescription medications.

√   And YOU WIN, because you can get started for the low fee and then let our automated system do almost everything for you. As you'll see, this gives you the most powerful way to achieve complete and total financial security... and hardly lift a finger.

CHAPTER THREE

Absolute Proof.

I filled my husband's two prescriptions at our local Hannaford store and I used my discount card. The first prescription's retail price was $62.99, but I only paid $13.55. The second prescription's retail price was $105.01 but I only paid $14.67 for a 90 day prescription. This was cheaper than the copay on my insurance card through my employer.

— Sonya Macdonald (South Paris, ME)

After losing my job and insurance, you came to my rescue by saving me hundreds of dollars!

— Peter West

MAKE MONEY HELPING PEOPLE

My name is Pauline Sims and my sister-in-law Sonya gave me a discount card while I saw her passing at Wal-Mart here in Columbia, SC. I had just finished shouting at the pharmacy guy telling him, "This is crazy if you think I'm going to pay $68.89 for this prescription!" So my sister-in-law told me to use the card and I did. Wow! Is all I can say. Get this! I paid only $17.64 for my prescription! How can I thank you!

— Ms. Pauline Sims (Columbia, SC)

I just received my free discount card from your company and thought this had to be a joke, but I would try it once. I had a prescription to get and it was gonna cost me $58.00 with my work insurance, but the drug store ran my cards and it was only $8.00. I couldn't believe it. I will keep using your discount cards and I keep telling everyone about it. THANK YOU.

— Kathy Cheesbro

I work at a clinic that treats MS, Parkinson's, Seizures, ALS, and numerous sleep disorders. I plan to distribute to my patients who are in need of assistance. A patient called in tears because she could not afford her medication. I searched and found this website. Using the discount card, she was able to afford her medication.

Amanda Swanson (Gloucester, VA)

Aloha, My name is Ed Nix. I am using the discount card because I have numerous prescriptions I purchase each month. I have saved considerable money because I am not carrying any insurance at all. I saved 30 dollars on one prescription and 65 dollars on another. I have seen discounts of several hundred dollars and more. I encourage you to check it out it's worth the comparison and why not save money right?

— Ed Nix (Aiea, HI)

MAKE MONEY HELPING PEOPLE

When I go to the pharmacy to pick up prescriptions, I always present 2 cards. My health insurance card and a free discount card off the Internet. I found pharmacies have different discounts for different insurance or discount cards. A person who does not use either one of these cards is overpaying for their prescriptions. I have been using my health insurance card to get discounts on prescriptions for my family. Recently, I have been experimenting with different services to try and find lower prices on prescription drugs. I was surprised when using a discount drug card printed off my computer at home for free was lower than using my health insurance card at the pharmacy. With my health insurance card I was paying $82.99 for 3 months of Kelnor 1/35, with the discount card it went down to $49.82. Another medication, Tretinoin 0.05% cream, I was paying $75.54, with the discount card $55.40. I saved $53.31 on these two medications by trying a discount prescription drug card instead of my health insurance card. The discount card might not always be lower in cost, but it is worth investigating. There is a healthcare crisis in this country. People want to use more healthcare products and services than they can afford. Our job as consumers is to find the lower cost ways of getting the products and services we value. I always present my health insurance and discount prescription drug card at the pharmacy for any medications I need. I ask the pharmacy to use which ever one costs less.

— H.G (New York, NY)

I recently picked up my dad's Torsemide at CVS and with our new discount card it was $5 for a 30-day supply. I said it should have been a 90-day supply and when they corrected the quantity the total cost was still only $5 and the retail price was over $70.

— Ronnie W.

MAKE MONEY HELPING PEOPLE

I didn't really think that the discount card would be useful until I went to the website and did a comparison. Not only did it save me over $50 on one of my medications, after doing the comparison I was able to save by paying cash for another. I am also going to be saving BIG on my wife's Rx.

— Ed P.

My wife and I befriended a gentleman approximately a year ago who had no health insurance but required medication because of a recent cranial procedure. We purchased his drugs for him at Walgreens at a cost of $297.00, but this time at renewal we visited our local pharmacy in town (Monroe) and saved a whopping $240.00. We recently found out about your organization and are informing several individuals that have no medical coverage. THANK YOU.

— Bruce L. (Glassboro, NJ)

I just had a personal incident occur that reinforces the value of the program! I had told my daughter back in Arkansas to be sure to call me before she refilled any prescriptions for the family. My son-in-law works for Entergy as an engineer and they have a $3,000 deductible health plan so their prescriptions are pretty much always out of pocket. My grandson takes the antibiotic Omnicef for ear infections and they have the script filled at Wal-Mart for around $80.00. She used the discount card for the refill and it cost her $25.43! When you consider the number of prescriptions filled annually by families (not to mention seniors) the potential economic impact is amazing. We owe it to our families and friends to get the card into their hands!

— Jerry D. Turney (Scottsdale, AZ)

Just an amazing program that does save you $$$!

— John Stanton

MAKE MONEY HELPING PEOPLE

At least one third of our patients are uninsured. They are mostly, really hard working guys that make too much money to qualify for medicaid, but they don't make enough to buy their own insurance. We have patients that take medication that doesn't work very well over a medication that they know works, but can't afford. These discount cards would be given to our patients that have no insurance, and are in need of some help. This is a great program. I must say, I'm very impressed.

— Gregory VillaBona, M.D. (Dover, DE)

I just want to say THANK YOU so much for sharing the savings card with me! With no health insurance, all of the medication required for my Lymes treatment is quite overwhelming, and this little card has saved me HUNDREDS of dollars in just the last three weeks! What a BLESSING!!

— Laurie D.

Greetings! Please permit me to first of all thank you for your discount pharmacy card. There are so many out there, but yours is the most helpful for patients who have dependency on medication!

— James Dennis

I really needed a CAT scan and couldn't afford it.
I was turned onto this discount card,
called the 1-800 number and with this card
I saved over $800. I couldn't believe it!

— Howard Donahue

I have always paid $40 for my 90-day supply
of meds. Today I went into the pharmacy
to pick it up and asked them to run the
discount card and my cost was only $13.47.
How nice was that!!!!! I say very nice. :)

— Theresa S.

MAKE MONEY HELPING PEOPLE

My friend is on a catastrophic plan without drug coverage and recently used this discount card and received a $55 discount without any hassle – super easy and he was very thankful. Thank you again for promoting the program at the last UBA conference! The cards look great and we have already distributed over 1000 of them!

— Allison Nickel, PHR Office Manager
at Albers & Company (Tacoma, WA)

I just recently moved to the United States and couldn't afford insurance. I have to say that I'm very thankful for this program that saved me more money that I could even imagine.

— Igor Matveev

Thank you, I was given this discount card and it helped me save on my prescriptions.

— Debra Wible

I decided to give your discount card a try. I had a prescription for something, I had sorta just been holding onto just for this reason. First, I went to your website and did a pharmacy location and price query. I found it to be just as simple and informative as when I had browsed around on it before. I chose to go to Wal-Mart because I figured every town has one and I was going there anyways. Once there, I asked the attendant for a price quote without the card. It came to around $30.00. Then, I presented the card and asked what the price would be with it. She looked at it and asked me if I could come back in about 10 minutes while she looked it up. I did and true to form, the price matched the website's quote of half off. On top of that, she had already filled it. I took that opportunity to ask her if she had ever seen or heard of this discount card before. She replied saying, "No, but I can tell you this, I've seen a lot of those so called discount cards before (rolling her eyes) and most aren't worth the trouble for people, but this one (handing it back to me)...this one's a good one." She then followed me down to the other end of the counter where the cashier was. At first, I thought it was a little odd cause she had left her post and there were other customers still waiting to be served. She put her hand on the cashier's shoulder and as I was paying for it, the cashier politely asked where I had obtained the card. I glanced at both of them and then the cashier explained, "I hope I'm not being too forward by asking you that, it's just that my sister is on a lot of medications and has no insurance...a card like that could really help her out." At that moment, I realized they must have talked about it. I told them that I had found you online, had spoken to you on the phone today and was trying the service out...that you were sending me more information and as soon as I could, I would be back with one for her sister. I am more excited about this more than ever before! The process is simple, the savings are unbelievable and the word of mouth alone could move these discount cards.

— John Baldwin (Virginia)

On Father's Day at my brother's house, his caretaker was there and she told a story of her mother who is being taken care of by a number of brothers and sisters of hers. Each month they get together to pay for her prescriptions. They pay about $260. So they were talking about how they had to get the money together and were waiting for a couple of the relatives to put their money up for this tremendous bill. When she took the discount card to the pharmacy and got the bill back, it was $116.

— Donald Hackney (Philadelphia, PA)

Thank you for giving me a chance
to be healthy and save me money!

— Frankie Wilson

MAKE MONEY HELPING PEOPLE

I am so excited about the savings on the Discount Card that I wanted to share with you. I don't have a prescription drug plan, so I thought I would give the discount card a try at the Wal-Mart pharmacy, thinking that it would save me $5 to $10 on a generic drug. The price that I have been paying is $54.62, and today with the discount card, my price is $29.57! And I thought that Wal-Mart would be the best discount until I did price comparison shopping online. I could have saved another dollar and not have the hassle of waiting in line if I had checked the comparison.

— Linda Allison (Jonesboro, AR)

As a small business owner and the rising cost of health insurance, your discount card helped me provide my employees with this great program and saved them a lot of money.

— Harry Porter

I just wanted to thank you so much for all your help. I just experienced these savings using your discount card. Using your card I paid $21.74 instead of my usual monthly payments of $369.00 for ANASTROZOLE TAB 1MG. You folks are a God send, keep up the good work and I'll be sure to tell my church group about the program.

— Sally F. (Victoria, TX)

I was on a city bus that crashed; I was injured and need to take pain medications regularly. I have to use my own cash for them and the insurance company reimburses me, and it can take some time... one of my meds I take was costing me $123.19 a month, and with the Discount card I paid $34.65. I saved $88.54! Another one was $142.99 retail and with the card I paid $85.05 saving $57.94! Thank You for what you are doing.

— Candice B.

MAKE MONEY HELPING PEOPLE

It was so easy. I went to the website,
printed a discount card, took it to
the pharmacy and saved $21.50.

— Sharon Jackson

I'm a diabetic and I have to take diabetic
medicine on a regular basis. Through the regular
insurance company, I was paying close to $140
for my prescription medicine – four different
medications. With the Discount card, now my
medication costs me $50, and $5 for shipping.

— Nelson Geralds (Pleasantville, NJ)

I do not have insurance I have been paying a lot
for my prescriptions. My pharmacist gave me
your discount card and my prescriptions were
half price. Thank you so much for helping me.

— Kent (PA)

Subway is my favorite fast food chain. The manager's husband has some heart issues and must take several prescriptions. Some were brands that don't have generic equivalents and we couldn't help her with those. But 3 or 4 prescriptions were for generics and the savings with the Discount card are about $60 a month – that's $720 more in their pocket every year.

— Brad Neillis (Spencer, TN)

Yesterday I met with a young man who could not afford the anti-rejection lab work he needs repeatedly since his liver transplant. These tests literally protect this 24-year-old man's life. I was so grateful to offer him free access to the services available through the Discount Card. His anti-rejection medication itself costs $800 a month. He told me, "You are doing a good thing." I had to fight back tears. This young man has no health insurance.

— Michael W. Ring (Bangor, ME)

MAKE MONEY HELPING PEOPLE

Just a quick story of interest. My wife hurt her foot today when a large table fell and hit the top of her foot. I took her to the emergency room and the physician said it was just a bad bruise. He gave her a prescription for 30 each 500mg tabs of Naprosyn, an anti-inflammatory. I checked the price on our link (we have a $25 deductible drug benefit on our US Airways health plan) and our discount price for this drug is $73.80 so that is a good deal for my $25 co-pay, right? I then checked for the generic equivalent Naroxen and found the following prices on my link... CVS: $14.64, Walgreens: $14.64, Fry's Grocery and several other grocery-based pharmacies: $7.85! I went to Fry's and bought it as a cash transaction! My savings were $25.00 - $7.85 = $17.15 and US Airways save a lot more than that! All for 5 min on the computer! This scenario is played out everyday with our clients!

— Jerry Turney (Scottsdale, AZ)

This is the best program ever. I can't believe you've done what our Government is still talking about. I saved so much money on my prescriptions and now all of my friends use this discount card. Great Job!!!

— Cindy Matthews

WOW! Just enjoyed great savings of $23.35 on my first try of the free healthcare savings card. I had to renew my anti-inflammatory 60-day supply. I presented the card and they punched in the discount code info on the front of the card. The prior amount of $52.49 (the so-called low price under my Cigna health plan) was somehow now magically only $23.35. And this discount card is FREE. I like this kind of math. Please let anyone know about this timely benefit.

— Mark P.

MAKE MONEY HELPING PEOPLE

I had one prescription that my prescription coverage only covered for 15 days. I was responsible for paying for the other 15 days of medication. And my out-of-pocket cost was $175 for those 15 days! So, I presented the discount card and was able to get it for an unbelievably low cost of $11.37 for a 90-day supply!

— Theresa Siderio

My mother takes an arthritis drug, but recently her plan stopped covering it. She was worried she'd have to switch to a less-effective drug or go without. Instead, she used the Discount card I gave her, and she saw big savings — even better than what her insurance previously covered.

— Brian Snyder, Communications Manager at UBA (Indianapolis, IN)

I was paying $164 for my wife Mary's medication and

now I pay $25. I was amazed and I'm thrilled to be saving so much money every month. It has made a big difference in our lives. I now use the discount card for all our medicine. I recommend that people use the pharmacy search engine to find the cheapest pharmacy in your area so you can start saving today.

— Joe Matthews (Maple Shade, NJ)

We are a prayer group here at Hope Clinic. I plan on giving these to Hope Clinic to give to their patients who are uninsured or under insured. This is why Hope Clinic got started. So people like that could get good healthcare based on their income. They are a non-profit organization. I was blessed with one of your discount cards that came in the mail. My husband used it first his medicine would have cost him $35.00 after discount it was just $13.24. I want to share our good fortune with others.

— Tammy Neville (Lafayette, TN)

MAKE MONEY HELPING PEOPLE

Two weeks ago on a Saturday I did a presentation about the discount card to a group of fifteen pastors. At the conclusion of the session one of the pastors wanted information about the Program but he also asked for one of my discount cards I was distributing. The following Monday (2 days later) he called and told me that right after the presentation he took a prescription to the pharmacy for a generic medicine LATANOPROST SOL for his wife. The pharmacy's system was down so they could not process the card. However, they told him to come back the next day and that if there was a discount they would refund him. Since his wife needed the medicine on Saturday, he went ahead and paid the $87.99 that he was accustomed to paying for the past year. The next day he went back as the pharmacy instructed so they would process the discount card to see if he were entitled to a discount. The card was processed and the pharmacy gave him a refund of $67.94! The new cost of the medicine with our card is now $20.05. The pastor told his congregation and they are waiting for a supply of cards to distribute that will bless so many people.

— Sandi Williams (Cheltenham, PA)

Being a single mother of 3 it's very difficult to make ends meet. The discount card helped me afford the medications I needed to keep my family healthy.

— Emily Hart

I have a friend who had a $65 copay on her son's medication and it was moving to $100 or more. I introduced her to the discount card and she found a pharmacy within 3 miles of her house where she could get the medication for $13.97... AMAZING! Not like the dozen other things I have seen come and go.

— Trebor N.

MAKE MONEY HELPING PEOPLE

I met a young girl about three weeks ago who has three young children. She was only 27 years old and had been taking the three children to the doctor for asthma for probably the last three months. And every time she'd go the doctor, the doctor prescribed medication that she cannot afford to buy. So we were talking about it and I said, "I may have a solution for you." So we went online to the website, put in the name of the medication and her zip code, and 2 of the 3 medicines went from $119.70 plus to $22.39, in that range. So, needless to say, this young mother with her 3 children, who had to make a decision between buying food or buying the children medicine; paying her rent or buying the children medicine, making sure they had the necessities of food and shelter…now she can actually have all three.

— Sandi Williams (Cheltenham, PA)

I usually pick up my dad's prescription drugs

at a local pharmacy. He is 92 years old, is enrolled in a Medicare Prescription Plan and has a special senior discount card so he rarely pays more than $7 to $10 for a 90-day supply of meds. However, he recently had a new, one-time prescription for a tiny tube of ointment that was not covered by anything he had. The price was $34, but with the card, he only paid $17.

— Ronnie Wolf (Cherry Hill, NJ)

I printed a discount card off the website and put it in my purse. I went to the local grocery store and ran into a friend who was there to fill a couple of prescriptions. I gave her the paper card I printed and told her to have the pharmacist check the price with the card and compare it to what she would normally pay. She saved $46.00 on two prescriptions that day using the discount card.

— Karen Kraft (Williamstown, MI)

MAKE MONEY HELPING PEOPLE

My wife was very sick recently and when she left the hospital she was given a prescription that was going to cost $93.00. When I gave the pharmacist my Discount card the price was only $71.00 with your discount.

— Herb (Atlanta, GA)

I thought I was doing well paying only the insurance copay of $15.00 for one of my wife's meds. Then I checked the Website and did a pharmacy search for the same med. Needless to say I was very happy to find that the pharmacy at my grocery store would only charge me $8.91. Thanks, you made my day.

— Bob Clemons (Toms River, NJ)

Wow, I saved so much on my prescriptions this month and I was able to go shopping for myself.

— Farrah Crest

I took my dog to the vet for his annual checkup, and the vet prescribed him 42 tablets of Cephalexin 500mg, 21 tablets of Enalapril 5mg, and 60 tablets of Levothyroxine 25mcg. The vet charged $32.58 for the Cephalexin, $23.76 for the Enalapril, and $68.72 for the Levothyroxine. With my discount card, I paid $10.58 for the Cephalexin (a savings of $22), $12.54 for the Enalapril (a savings of $11.22), and $12.44 for the Levothyroxine (a savings of $56.28). I saved $89.50 total! Finally, when I went to the doctor, I was prescribed Bactrim DS 800-160. My insurance didn't cover it, and I would've had to pay $76.28 for the generic, but with my discount card, I paid $11.26, saving me $65.

— Krisin Milana (Lindenwold, NJ)

Thank you. I was able to save $69.74 on just one medication wow what a blessing.

— George Nelson (Mullica Hill, NJ)

MAKE MONEY HELPING PEOPLE

I get a prescription filled every month at Walgreens for my parrot. I usually pay $11.00 and with your discount card I only pay $7.00.

— Dwight (Las Vegas, NV)

I am senior pastor at My Liberty Church of God and Christ located in Philadelphia, PA in the West Oak Lane section of the city. I pastor about 4,000 people here at the church. The first week after I gave the Discount card out to my congregation, I got numerous phone calls from the members of the church that they went to the pharmacy, used their Card and had a discount on their prescription. I was amazed. Our church was able to help our members get some discounts where they can be able to manage and budget their money and do other things.

— Bishop Earnest E. Morris, Sr. (Philadelphia, PA)

People just can't believe that they can get such fantastic savings for free. Today people are growing in excitement over this discount card because of their experiences. People see me on the street and in other places. They come over and hug me and thank me for giving them this card. This card has been a blessing to a lot of people who every month are trying to decide whether they should buy their groceries or buy their prescriptions. And with this discount card, those folks can buy groceries AND buy prescriptions, and it's really helping them in life.

— Joseph Yeoman, Sr. (Pleasantville, NJ)

Thank you for your discount prescription medication cards – our patients will greatly benefit from this program I'm sure.

— Pam Moella, Community Clinic of Door County (Sturgeon Bay, WI)

MAKE MONEY HELPING PEOPLE

With this discount card, people are now finding out they can make a choice to be able to get money back into their homes, to be able to do some of those things that they desire to do, without spending all their money on medications. They are so excited because it's actually saving them money, and when they realize it's free, they can't believe this discount card could actually save them hundreds and hundreds of dollars.

— Cathy Dunkin (Philadelphia, PA)

CHAPTER FOUR

How Our Program Works.

You will use our 20-Second System to process mail that introduces our exciting and proven Passive Income Fundraising Program to the groups. Each group is issued a special fundraising code and an initial batch of 5,000 DISCOUNT PRESCRIPTION CARDS they can give out. Then every prescription purchase that comes in with this code is credited to you and the group. They receive $1.50 every time each one of their friends and family members use our savings cards, and you earn 35 cents. (More on how this can pay you huge commissions in just a bit...)

The groups introduce our DISCOUNT

PRESCRIPTION CARDS to their friends and family by sending emails or passing out the cards we provide to them. This tells their supporters about our unique fundraising program and makes them want to participate. It gives them the website address and the special fundraising code they can use when they visit their local pharmacy and fill their prescriptions.

Each time they use the groups code to purchase an authorized prescription, the group gets paid, and so do you! Sending out some emails or passing out our fundraising cards to the supports of the group makes it so easy for all kinds of groups to raise the money they need.

These groups include: School groups, church groups, 4-H groups, youth programs, women groups, Bible study groups, senior groups, veterans groups, all types of business groups and many more...

Any non-profit organization that wants to raise money to help pay for their various activities can benefit from our Passive Income Fundraising Program. And your only requirement is to use our 20-Second System to process mail that introduces this to the groups.

The supporters of the group will love our DISCOUNT PRESCRIPTION CARD that lets them save big money on all of their medications. Earlier I gave you a few very extreme examples of some of our cardholders who have saved as much as 98.12% on their prescription medications. That sounds so unbelievable, and yet it's true! Our cardholders have saved 80%... 85%... 93% to as much as 98.12% off of the cost of their prescription drugs!

And yet, those are extreme examples. So let me give you some other real-life prescriptions that our cardholders saved money on over the last few months:

MAKE MONEY HELPING PEOPLE

Drug Type	Retail Price	Member Paid	Savings	Pharmacy
Efficient	$580.99	$330.45	43.12%	Super Fresh
Cialis	$164.99	$132.35	9.78%	Walgreens
Phentermine	$35.20	$10.49	70.19%	Smith's
Carisoprodol	$34.69	$21.72	37.38%	Walgreens
Amphetamine	$131.64	$66.00	49.86%	Sam's Club
Tramadol	$30.99	$8.77	71.70%	Wellstar
Estradiol	$80.99	$52.31	35.41%	Walgreens
Pantoprazole	$109.99	$17.98	83.65%	Target
Guanfacine	$271.51	$15.99	94.11%	Walmart
Cheratussin	$17.89	$10.25	42.70%	CVS
Propanol	$79.99	$14.00	82.49%	Rite Aid
Cymbalta	$267.69	$238.36	10.95%	Osco Drug
Hydromorphone	$132.99	$55.99	57.89%	Target
Novolog	$510.99	$438.86	14.11%	Winn-Dixie
Bupropion	$109.99	$23.61	78.53%	Vons

These 15 examples came from a recent commission report for just one of the people who is already making money. There were a total of 774 prescriptions on this one affiliate report. I wanted to pull a few of them to show you some of the average savings. As you can see, the group members and their supporters can save a lot of money, so they'll keep using their prescription discount card, again and again...

And Each Time They Use It
the Group and You Can Get Paid!

Most pharmacies keep the customer's DISCOUNT PRESCRIPTION CARD on file (just like their insurance card) and reference it each time that same customer fills a new prescription... to make sure the customer always gets the lowest price... And you can get paid over and over again – even if the customer doesn't remember to bring their card with them!

Yes, they give their card to
the pharmacy once, and...

You Can Get Paid for Many Years
from Every Person Who Uses
Their Discount Prescription Card!

It's the perfect way for the groups to raise all the money they want. All they do is pass out our DISCOUNT PRESCRIPTION CARD to all of their friends, family and other supporters. This makes it super easy for the people who support their group to see the tremendous value of saving up to 87% or more off on all of their prescriptions and help the group raise money. Best of all, every card user can result in ever-increasing profits for you!

Here's How You Make Money:

A.   You get our Easy Passive Income
        System for a very low cost. This lets you

cash-in with our copyrighted system for processing mail to non-profit groups. This makes it SO EASY for each non-profit group who signs up to raise all the money they desperately need.

B. The group gets $1.50 every time one of their DISCOUNT PRESCRIPTION CARDS is used to purchase a prescription drug.

C. As an Affiliate, you also get paid 35 cents for every DISCOUNT PRESCRIPTION CARD that's used. Yes, you get paid each time it's used. That may not seem like a lot, but wait until you see how this could potentially add up to many hundreds or even thousands of dollars a month!

D. You'll use our copyrighted 20-

second processing system that introduces our program to the groups who need to RAISE MONEY for their group activities.

E. The group passes out their DISCOUNT PRESCRIPTION CARD to all of their supporters. They can also instruct supporters to visit their Fundraising Website (included with the program) and download a printable card right from their website.

F. The supporters use our savings card each time they get a prescription filled, to make sure they're always getting the absolute best price.

G. The group gets a fast and simple way to raise the money they need.

H. And you get paid a passive income...

every month... over and over again!

I.   There's no cap on how much you can get paid.

J.   We are happy to do everything for you, because the more we can do to see to it that you get paid the largest amount of money, the more we make for ourselves.

And best of all...

You Simply Use Our EASY PASSIVE INCOME SYSTEM to Introduce This Amazing Program to the Groups.

We run the whole thing for you. You simply use our Easy Passive Income System to introduce this program to the non-profit groups. Then let us do the rest. This takes a few minutes a day and you're done. And yet, for this few minutes a day, you're getting the opportunity to potentially make more money than most people make working full time.

Yes, all it takes is a small amount of time each to do the one step to introduce the non-profit groups who need our program. And yet THIS FIRST STEP is VITAL because it sets up the other steps and lets us work with the groups.

We do everything else:

1.   We work closely with the groups...

2.   The company we have partnered with updates their list of approved pharmacies (54,000 pharmacies and counting) and the pre-negotiated discount prices for all the pharmaceuticals every 24 hours – through a handy tool right on the website that you and all of your

fundraising groups will receive.

3.   This company will take care of all of the customer service issues. There is a hotline phone number on each card that lets them take calls from the patients and pharmacies.

4.   We work with the groups and their members to make sure they have EVERYTHING they need to raise all the money they want.

And the most exciting thing we do for you is the fact that...

We Do All of This for You for a Very Low One-Time Fee and Then We Will Continue to Do All We Can to Make Sure That You Keep Getting Paid the Largest Sum of Money.

Anybody can say they want to help you

make the largest sum of money and all other business opportunities do say things like this. And yet, how many of the people who "claim" they want to help you make money are ready, willing and able to spend large amounts of their own money and other valuable resources in an attempt to make sure that you get paid the largest sum of money? Very few. And yet, this is what we do for you 7 days a week, 365 days a week!

All you are doing is the first step. The other steps are done for you at our expense, not yours. And the more we do to make money for you and the groups, the more money we make for ourselves.

Isn't this the way an honest and ethical business should operate?

YES IT IS!!!

Listen, getting this type of help, support and guidance from joint venture partners who make money for a percentage of all the money they make for you is something that you only get from the very expensive business opportunities. It's something that you usually have to spend tens of thousands of dollars to receive. And yet, you are not being asked to spend thousands of dollars to become a Representative of our Easy Passive Income System... You won't even pay a tiny fraction of that price to get involved in this opportunity...

Instead, your only cost is a low one-time fee to become a Representative of our Easy Passive Income System. Just cover this fee and we'll help you become an Affiliate for our health technology partner. Then we'll rush our complete start-up materials that make it easy for you to help us introduce our revolutionary fundraising program to the non-profit groups.

For this very low start-up cost...

You will enjoy the benefits of an expensive business opportunity, such as a franchise, without the high cost and headaches and hassles. You now have the greatest chance to make money, by helping the largest number of people.

"Our Complete Program has the Power to
Give You an AUTOMATIC INCOME
That Can Keep Coming to You for Years."

As you probably know, in business it's not legal to guarantee anyone will make any specific sum of money. Not even the most proven business opportunities like the McDonald's restaurants (which has made hundreds of people millionaires and multi millionaires) can promise that you will make any specific sum of money. So I can't promise or guarantee that you will make many tens of thousands or even hundreds of thousands of dollars a year. And yet, having said all of this, I can promise...

The Potential Power to Make Huge Sums
of Passive Income is Now Yours.

Remember – according to The Kaiser Family

Foundation – doctors wrote over 4 billion prescriptions for drugs in America last year alone. That's an average of roughly 13 prescriptions for each man, woman and child each year! But for the sake of all of our examples, we're going to show you how much money you could potentially make if each family were to use our savings card to fill just one prescription a month.

So How Much Can You Make? Hold On... Because the Answer May Shock You!

First, here's the amount of commissions that are paid each time the group members and the supporters of the group use our DISCOUNT PRESCRIPTION CARD to fill a prescription.

The Group Gets Paid	You Get Paid	We Get Paid
$1.50	$0.35	$0.10

As you can see, we also get paid a small amount of money (a dime) every time one of these people purchases a prescription using the

DISCOUNT PRESCRIPTION CARD. And because of that fact...

We Have the Ultimate Reason to Do Everything
We Can to Help the Groups and You
Make the Maximum Amount of Money.

Second, using our system to attract the groups who need to make money is easy. It takes around 20 seconds per group. And this small activity can get you hundreds or even thousands of people who are using our cards to save money on all of their prescriptions. This Chart is proof:

CHART #1

Number of Groups	Number of Members in Each Group Who are Participating	Total Number of Cardholders
10	30	300
25	30	750
75	30	2,250
100	30	3,000

Now let's see the amount of money you could potentially make when the groups get involved in our program. This next chart is based on 3 things: #1. The group getting paid a $1.50 commission per prescription filled. #2. An average of 1 prescription filled per family each month. #3. Each member handing out an average of 10 cards:

CHART #2

Total Group Members	Number of Free Cards	Average Monthly Prescriptions Filled	Monthly Income for the Group	Monthly Income for You
30	300	300	$450	$105
50	500	500	$750	$175
100	1,000	1,000	$1,500	$350
250	2,500	2,500	$3,750	$875
500	5,000	5,000	$7,500	$1,750
1,000	10,000	10,000	$15,000	$3,500

* Your own income will vary. This is not a guarantee that you will earn any specific sum of money. However, as you've seen, just a handful of groups could potentially put many thousands of dollars in your pocket!

In fact:

Just a Few Groups Who are Deeply Committed
to Our Passive Income Fundraising Program
Could Potentially Pay You Thousands
of Dollars Each and Every Month!

Yes, it's potentially possible to get paid
thousands of dollars from just a few groups who
received just one of pieces of mail that you
process and then lets us work closely with them
over a period of time. Remember, You are being
paid in the ultimate way: from the combined
efforts of many other people. And as with any
legitimate home business, there can be no
promise or guarantee that you will earn any
specific sum of money...

This could potentially pay many thousands
of dollars from just one group. And it's money
that can continue to be paid to you – for years.

CHAPTER FIVE

You Could Enjoy Success with Just a Handful of Groups!

Getting paid a percentage of the money for all of the work that is done for you by our company and the groups (who are using our program to raise money) is the secret that makes this Easy Passive Income System superior to every other business opportunity. This is an honest and legitimate way to make money without your direct effort. It's the same advantage that all of the most successful people in the world have... and now it's yours!

Just let our 20-Second Mail Processing System introduce our Program to the groups.

This is all you do. The total time to process the mail for each group is only 20-seconds. And it's so simple and easy a 10-year old child can do it.

Your total time can be as little as a few short minutes a day. After that, you will have the ability to sit back, relax, shop, fish, spend time with your kids or grandkids, work on your hobby, or sleep – AND STILL MAKE MONEY. Remember, all of the selling and ongoing customer service work with each individual group who signs up under you will be done for you.

And because of this...

You Could Get Paid... for Years...
for a Small Number of Groups.

It's potentially possible to get paid a huge automatic income from just a handful of groups who gets the mail you process and then let us work closely with them. Yes, you simply spend a few enjoyable minutes a day using our Easy Passive Income System to process the mail that is designed to introduce the groups to our unique program and then get paid a huge automatic income that can keep coming to them and you for many months and even years!

So GO BACK and STUDY the two charts...

YOU'LL SEE: As a mathematical example only (to show you the powerful potential of this home-based business) all it would take is 10 groups who received one of the pieces of mail you processed with our copyrighted 20-second system and then got involved in our revolutionary program, to get paid thousands of dollars a month.

Study the charts. You'll see, as an example only, let's say you use our Easy Passive Income System to sign up only 10 groups who each had

25 members who passed out 10 DISCOUNT PRESCRIPTION CARDS to their friends and family members. When that happens, and each cardholder fills an average of 1 prescription a month, the group would get paid $3,750!

That's great news for the group! After all, they just got paid $3,750 a month and they never had to go through all of the headaches and hassles of most fundraising programs.

But it's even better for YOU, because in this example...

You Would Also Get Your Own
Passive Monthly Check for $875...
And You Did Almost Nothing!

That's not a promise or guarantee that you will make that amount or any specific sum... But who knows? Your groups could pass out even more DISCOUNT PRESCRIPTION CARDS or have even a higher-than-average number of prescriptions filled each month.

I cannot, and will not, promise that this home-based business will make you $875 a month in pure passive income or any specific sum. But as the mathematical example proves, the potential to get paid as much as $875 a month in passive income or much more is definitely here.

After all, this figure is based on only 10 groups who had 25 members who were passing out our DISCOUNT PRESCRIPTION CARDS to 10 of their friends and family (who were then using our savings card to fill an average of just 1 prescription a month). If that were to happen, you would get paid $875 a month in pure passive income.

Does that sound exciting?

GREAT! It really should. After all, in this

example, what did you do to get paid this money? Very little. All you did was used our complete Easy Passive Income System to introduce our program to 10 groups of only 25 members each, who passed our DISCOUNT PRESCRIPTION CARDS to 10 of their friends and family members. When these people used our savings card to fill an average of 1 prescription a month, you just got paid $875.

If those numbers held out, that money would keep coming to you every month!

But what if you'd like more than $875 a month?

What if you wanted to make as much as $50,000... to $75,000... and even as much as $100,000 a year or even more?

Is that possible?

Well, let's take a look. Let's say you were

using our Easy Passive Income System to introduce our program to bigger groups, with more than 25 participating members. Let's say you had groups of as many as 100 or even 250 members each who were passing these free savings cards out to all of their friends and family members. Can you picture that? GOOD! Okay, let's do the math: Let's say you had just 10 groups of 150 members each, who gave our free DISCOUNT PRESCRIPTION CARDS to 10 of their friends and family members. How much would you make then? Well, the answer is very exciting! Because when that happened, and when these people used our savings card to fill an average of 1 prescription a month...

You Just Got Paid $5,250 a Month.

That's $63,000 a year!

And what did you do to get paid all this money?

That's the super exciting part! Because once you used our system to introduce our fundraising program to all of the groups, you would have to do virtually nothing! The group members pass the free savings cards to their friends and family members and when all of these people (in the mathematical example on the last page) use their cards an average of once a month, your annual income would come to a whopping sixty three thousand dollars.

But don't stop here!

Because it's easy to see that the potential to make a lot more than $63,000 a year is definitely here.

So with that in mind, let me ask...

Would You Like to Get Paid as Much as $100,000 a Year in Passive Income?

If so, let's do that math: If you had just 20

groups of 150 members each, who passed our free DISCOUNT PRESCRIPTION CARDS to 10 of their friends and family members and when these people used our savings card to fill an average of 1 prescription a month, you just got paid $10,500 a month, or $126,000 a year.

See how easy it is to figure out the money you could potentially make?

Good! Because you can see how possible it is to put yourself in position to get paid as much as $5,250 to $10,500 a month or even more?

Okay, then please do your own math. Weigh it all out. Consider everything we've gone over. Think deeply about how much good our Easy Passive Income System does for so many people. Then create your own mathematical charts and consider how much money you could potentially make for various numbers of groups who are using our DISCOUNT PRESCRIPTION CARDS to raise the money they need. Do this and you'll see, the potential to get paid huge sums of money is definitely here. I can't promise that you'll get paid as much as $63,000 to $126,000 a year or any specific amount and am not showing you these examples as a promise that you will make any specific amount of money. The amount of commissions you get paid will be based on the number of your non-profit groups that we will be working with (for you), how many savings cards they pass out, and how many people use the cards to purchase their prescriptions. Your results will vary based on many factors, and so I can't guarantee you'll make any specific sum of money.

But I am Making You These Promises:

I PROMISE: It is possible to make $100,000 a year or more, by using our 20-second system to process mail that introduces our Passive Income Fundraising Program to the non-profit groups and letting them and us do the rest.

I PROMISE: We will do all we can to help you make the largest amount of money, because the more money you make, the more we make.

I PROMISE: You can get started for a very low one-time fee.

I PROMISE: You will get everything you need to make money part-time.

I PROMISE: My staff and I will always be here for you.

I PROMISE: This lets you make money and help so many other people.

In fact, when you add it all up, you'll realize...

No Other Home-Based Business
Lets You Make So Much Money...
Do So Much Good... for So Many People...
with Such Little Time and Effort.

I PROMISE: This is completely moral – ethical – and even fun!

I PROMISE: You will get the same type of benefits of a very expensive franchise that costs as much as $50,000 to $100,000 or more.

Yes, for a low one time start-up fee, you will receive the same type of valuable services that franchise opportunities offer to their franchisees, for tens of thousands of dollars. That may sound hard to believe right now, but stay with me and I'll prove it to you!

I PROMISE: After you do the 1 very small, but vital step, our company – the DISCOUNT

PRESCRIPTION CARD company – and the groups do all of the work for you.

I PROMISE: This is totally private, you will never talk with anyone.

I PROMISE: You can get a lifetime of residual income.

I PROMISE: This is completely different than any other home business. It contains the greatest features of a very expensive franchise, for a fraction of the cost.

With All This Said, It's Time to
Wrap This Chapter Up...

By now you (hopefully) know: this may quite possibly be the greatest money-making program ever developed because it lets us make our money by helping so many other people...

A.   We're giving the supporters of each group a great bargain. Remember, the consumers who own our discount prescription cards have already saved a total of $179,109,815 off the regular prices of the prescription drugs they need. And now people can use our absolutely free DISCOUNT PRESCRIPTION CARD and save up to 87% on their medications and help the group raise money every time they get a prescription filled.

B.   We're helping YOU make all the money you want... It's what we do!

C.   We're helping each group raise all the money they need...

So many people benefit greatly from this program... So many lives can be changed. This separates our Program from all the others...

For a very low start-up cost, you will enjoy the benefits of an expensive business opportunity, such as a franchise, without the high cost and headaches and hassles. You now have the greatest chance to make money, by helping the largest number of people.

This is different and better than any other moneymaking program you have ever seen. However, you may still have a few doubts. So read on and let me answer this one final question you may still be asking yourself...

CHAPTER SIX

How Much is This Worth?

I believe this is the greatest way that average people can make a HUGE full-time income for only doing something part-time. It beats every other business opportunity we've ever seen. And I'm talking about businesses that sell for up to $50,000 and more. That may be the boldest statement ever, but read on and let me prove it to you...

ABSOLUTE PROOF of Why I Firmly Believe Our Easy Passive Income System That Lets You Make Money in as Little as 10 Minutes a Day is Worth as Much as $50,000 to $100,000 or More.

As you may recall, one of MY PROMISES I made to you is the fact that you will get the same type of benefits of a very expensive franchise that costs as much as $50,000 to $100,000 or more. That may be the boldest statement I've made so far! So please read closely and let me tell you why it is true.

For starters, a franchise is simply a business opportunity that provides people with three things they need to make money:

1.   A proven and unique opportunity that is already making money.

2.   A detailed System that is easy to understand and simple to use.

3.   Continuous help, support, and guidance from experts who understand all aspects of the business.

When somebody invests in a Franchise, they get all 3 of these things.

It sounds so simple, and yet these three ingredients are largely responsible for one of the world's most lucrative industries that generates well over $1,000,000,000,000 (ONE TRILLION DOLLARS) every year. And that is GOOD NEWS FOR YOU, because this is what you will have when you get involved in our totally revolutionary Passive Income System that's designed to let you get paid every time somebody uses our DISCOUNT PRESCRIPTION CARD to save up to 87% on all of their FDA approved medications.

We know that most Franchise opportunities are very expensive.

In fact, many Franchises cost $150,000 to $200,000 or more. Some people even pay millions of dollars for this type of business.

So why are these people willing to spend so much money for these opportunities?

That's simple...

When You Buy a Franchise, You are Almost Guaranteed to Greatly Succeed.

Yes, it's true...

According to the U.S. Department of Commerce, 95% of all Small Businesses fail in the first 5 years. But Franchises are different. Over 85% of all Franchises succeed!

Think about that...

√   Regular Small Business: 95% FAIL within 5 years.

√   Franchise Opportunity: 85% SUCCEED.

Isn't that exciting! Over 95% of regular small businesses fail within 5 years...

But 85% of Franchises succeed.

Pretty amazing, huh?

But there's one problem: Most people don't have $150,000 to a million dollars to invest in a Franchise – even if it's proven. And that's GREAT NEWS FOR YOU, because now you can get started for the an amazingly low price that will blow you away!

This amazing home business opportunity lets you profit by helping so many people so many ways. Remember: The 3 components of our Easy Passive Income System are: #1. Helping groups raise huge sums of money without the headaches and hassles most fundraisers require. #2. Helping people save money on their prescription medications. #3. And paying YOU huge sums of passive income!

If you studied the two Charts I gave you in this section, you know:

You Could Get Paid... for Many Years... from a Small Number of Groups.

I did my best to prove all of this to you. But now we're running out of time.

So let me summarize this with 5 important facts:

FACT #1: This gives you the power to get paid a huge passive income from a handful of groups who receives the mail you process and then let us work closely with them.

FACT #2: You spend a few minutes a day using our Easy Passive Income System to process the mail that is designed to introduce the groups to our unique program and then get paid a passive income that can keep coming to you for many months and even years!

FACT #3: As the mathematical examples we gave you revealed: all it would take is 10 groups who received one of the pieces of mail you processed with our copyrighted 20-second system and then got involved in our program, to get paid up to thousands of dollars a month.

FACT #4: You have seen how this could potentially pay you $875 each and every month for only a small number of groups who were using our Passive Income Fundraising Program to raise all of the money they need for all of their group activities. For example: If you were to use our simple 20-Second Processing System to introduce this to only 10 groups who each had 25 members and they passed out 10 DISCOUNT PRESCRIPTION CARDS to their friends and family members, and each cardholder fills an average of 1 prescription a month, the groups would get $3,750 a month and you would get paid $875 a month.

The numbers don't lie.

You Would Get Paid $875 a Month – Every Month – in Pure Massive Income.

All four of those facts are super exciting! But the final fact is your icing on your cake...

FACT #5: You have also seen how it is possible to make $100,000 a year or more, by using our 20-second system to process mail that introduces our Passive Income Fundraising Program to the non-profit groups and letting them and us do the rest. As you have seen, we will do all we can to help you make the largest amount of money, because the more money you make, the more we make. Remember, as an example only: If you had just 20 groups of 150 members each, who passed our free DISCOUNT PRESCRIPTION

CARDS to 10 of their friends and family members and when these people used our savings card to fill an average of 1 prescription a month, you just got paid $10,500 a month, or $126,000 a year in totally passive income.

As you know, I can't promise that you will get paid as much as $126,00 a year or any specific amount. The examples I have given you are not a promise or guarantee that you will make any specific amount. I hope you understand this. The amount of commissions you can get paid with our Easy Passive Income System will be based on the number of your non-profit groups that we will be working with (for you), how many savings cards they pass out, and how many people use the cards to purchase their prescriptions. Your actual results will vary based on many factors, and I can't promise or guarantee you'll make any specific amount of money.

But having said all that, you also know:

> The potential to get paid huge sums of money is definitely here!

> This lets you make money and rewards you for helping so many other people.

> And when you add it all up, you'll realize that no other home-based business lets you make so much money and do so much good for so many people.

> As you've seen, this is completely moral – ethical – and even fun! Plus, this gives you all of the same type of benefits of a very expensive franchise that costs as much as $50,000 to $100,000 or more.

> And finally, this is totally private. You

will never have to talk with anyone. Our company, the DISCOUNT PRESCRIPTION CARD company – and the groups do all of the work for you.

And when you add it all up, you'll realize that, as hard as it may to have believed in the beginning, this really does give you...

The Power to Stay Home Each Day
and Get a Huge Passive Income.

This is your opportunity to make money without your direct effort. It's the same advantage that all of the most successful people have... and now it's yours!

Two of our closest friends and business advisors don't want us to sell this complete Easy Passive Income System. They want to help us franchise it and offer each franchise for at least $25,000. That's still a fraction of the price that many franchises charge. We thought about doing this. But then we changed our mind (at least for now).

First, we want as many people as possible to have this opportunity. And I may be wrong, but I don't think too many people who will respond to this offer can afford $25,000 – even for a legitimate opportunity that is this powerful.

Second, our company also receives a small percentage of every dollar you make.

So because of these two things – I'm not charging $25,000. Or even $7,500. I'm not even going to ask for $1,000. Instead, you'll get the complete Easy Passive Income System for a very low one-time fee.

How it works: Go through the rest of this book to discover more about this powerful way to stay home and make money. Then follow the simple instructions in the last chapter. The complete information will be sent to you absolutely free. Then, if you are still excited about this opportunity, my staff and I will sign you up as an Affiliate for our revolutionary health technology partner that is the foundation of our Easy Passive Income System.

I'll make it easy and inexpensive for you to become a Representative of our complete Easy Passive Income System. Then my staff and I will enroll you as an Affiliate for the health technology company who is providing the Prescription Savings Cards. We'll make sure they send your 5,000 custom-printed Discount Prescription Cards directly to you. This lets you cash-in with everything you've discovered in this book.

So please go through the rest of this book. Then follow the instructions in the last chapter and let me hear from you at once.

SECTION TWO

The Power of Direct Response Marketing.

CHAPTER SEVEN

Why Our Marketing System is the Ultimate Way for You to Stay Home and Make Huge Sums of Money.

There is only one step for making money with our complete Easy Passive Income System. This step involves you using our 20-second system to process mail that introduces our Fundraising Program to the non-profit groups. From that point forward, you will let the group, our company and our health technology partner do the rest.

You can count on us to do all we can to help

you make the largest amount of money, because the more money you make, the more we make. I gave you an example in the last chapter to show you the kind of money that's potentially possible. Here it is again: if you had just 20 groups of 150 members each, who used the methods we give them to pass out our free DISCOUNT PRESCRIPTION CARDS to 10 of their friends and family members and if these people used our savings card to fill an average of 1 prescription a month...

You Would Get Paid $10,500 a Month
or $126,000 a Year in Passive Income.

Of course, that's potential, not promised income. Nobody can ethically and legally promise that you will get paid as much as $126,00 a year or any specific amount, and that's not what I'm doing with these examples. However, the examples in this book are your proof that you really could potentially get paid a six figure annual income. Best of all, it's easy to figure out how much money you could make. Just study the charts in Section One. The amount of commissions you can get paid with our Easy Passive Income System are based on the number of your non-profit groups that we will be working with (for you), how many savings cards they pass out, and how many people use the cards to fill their prescriptions. Your actual results will vary based on many factors, and we can't promise or guarantee you'll make any specific amount. But having said all that, you also know, the potential to get paid huge sums of money is definitely here.

This is your opportunity to make money without your direct effort. It's the same advantage that all of the most successful people have... and now it's yours! As you'll see, our marketing system is so easy to understand and use a 12-year-old child can make money with it! Because of this, it only takes a few minutes of training before you're ready to make money.

The fact that this Marketing System is simple lets you get off to the most powerful and profitable start. You can get started fast and have the power of momentum working for you from day one!

This is especially important, because...

Most Marketing Plans are Very Complicated.

The most successful multi-million dollar marketing plans can take a long time to learn. They are difficult to set up and run. This makes it hard to get off to a profitable start.

Bill Gates, one of the world's most famous billionaires says:

"If My Staff Can't Write a Basic Business and Marketing Plan on a Single Sheet of Paper – I Won't Do It!"

This man understands. So do we!

Simplicity is power. The simpler something is, the easier it is to get started and succeed.

Our marketing system is simple and easy... And yes, we have put it all on a single sheet of paper.

But There's One Major Problem.

Here it is: On the surface, this system seems way too simple and easy. The danger is that you'll think it's too simple. If that happens, you won't value or appreciate all the hard work it took to carefully build this for you.

So in the rest of this chapter (and the final two chapters) I'll tell you about some of the main elements that have gone into this very powerful, but simple system. It's important to know about these things. Otherwise, you'll never fully understand and appreciate all we're doing to see to it that you make the largest sum of money.

So please read carefully. And consider this:

"The Why is Always More
Important Than the How."

The dictionary defines "why" as the cause or reason behind something. The word "how" is the way you do it.

The most brilliant thinkers have told us that the why to do something is always more important than how to do it. So let's spend some quality time talking about the different elements that have gone into this powerful marketing system. Shall we?

OKAY, for starters...

Think of Our Marketing System as If It
Were a True Money Machine That You Can
Use to Crank Out Large Amounts of Cash!

This Machine Has Been Carefully
Built for You. Now All You Have to Do is
Punch One Button to Crank Out the Money.

The "money machine" is a great analogy for our Easy Passive Income System. Why? Because this entire program has been built to let us do all the complicated things that must be done to crank out the largest amount of money by providing the largest amount of value for the most people. However, all you do is one step. This is a simple step. It's so easy to do. But it's a vital step that must be done before any money can be made.

You must know just how important this step is before you can appreciate it.

So here we go.

First, a quote from one of my mentors:

"Marketing Takes a Day to Learn
and a Lifetime to Master."

This is so true.

You see, there's only two basic steps behind every great marketing plan:

STEP ONE: Attracting the very best prospects for whatever you're offering.

STEP TWO: All the activities you must go through to sell and re-sell the largest number of these people the things they really want.

That's it. This is the essence of all marketing. It's simply doing all the things you can to attract the very best prospects, sell them, make sure they stay happy, and do more business with them for the longest time.

You'll use our proven system to take care of the first step (which introduces the groups to our Passive Income Fundraising Program). Our company and our health technology partner take care of the second step. Best of all, our powerful sales materials and our staff do all the work for you. You'll be thrilled when you realize how easy this is.

But Don't Let the Ease and Simplicity
of This One Step Fool You.

You will be playing a vital role in our marketing process. The step you do is vital to your success and ours. All of the basics behind this will be totally clear by the time you finish going through this book. By the end of this book, you will be excited because you'll have a deeper understanding and appreciation of all the various marketing elements that have gone into this very simple system.

So relax. You may only want to know the "how" to do it part of our system, but the "why" it works is much more important. The more you know about the why it works, the more successful you will be.

Here are the 2 main reasons why I believe that this marketing system is the ultimate way to make money:

1.   This is built on proven Direct Response Marketing methods that have brought us tens of millions of dollars.

2.   The one step you do is vital to both of us. This lets me put all of my company's

time and energy into the second step, which is made up of all the things that must be done to introduce our Passive Income Fundraising Program to the non-profit groups that you will be attracting and make sure they stay happy and continue using our program to raise all the money they need for all of their group activities.

As you will see, letting YOU focus on doing the first step, with us putting our time and attention on the second step – is the ultimate win/win partnership between you, my company and our health technology partner.

Here are 5 major advantages for you to consider:

1.   All you do is one step.

2.   The sales materials, our expert staff,

and our health technology partner who provides the DISCOUNT PRESCRIPTION CARDS, do all the work for you.

3.   You will never do any personal selling or even talk with a single person.

4.   Our success is directly tied to yours.

      We are in the powerful position to make many thousands of dollars for doing all we can to help you deposit large sums of money into your bank account! We get paid HUGE profits for the help we give you. Plus, as you saw in the first section, we get a small percentage of on-going profits for every dollar we help you make.

5.   This gives you many powerful advantages that the people who are

already making thousands of dollars a month don't have.

Add it up. You'll see. These five advantages give you the ultimate way to stay home and make huge sums of money.

All this will be made perfectly clear to you as you go through the rest of this book... But for now, it is very important to know that the fact that we will continue to be rewarded to help you make money is just one more major advantage you'll have over all of the other people who are already making thousands of dollars a month.

So now let's move on.

In the next chapter, I'll tell you about the 2 major mistakes that all of the people who are already making tens of thousands of dollars a month are making. I'll go over each mistake very carefully. Then I'll tell you how our complete system eliminates each mistake. Read this chapter right now.

CHAPTER EIGHT

Here are the 2 Major Mistakes Everyone is Making and How Our System Eliminates Each One.

Making a lot of money is very simple. In fact, it's so simple, most people over-think it and never become financially independent.

You don't have to be one of these people.

Here's all you have to:

A.   Find average people who are making

huge amounts of money.

B.   Learn all their secrets. Do whatever you can to find out what they're doing right and wrong.

C.   Then duplicate their actions. Just do more of the things they're doing right and develop a powerful solution that eliminates each of their major mistakes.

The world's most expensive marketing expert (Jay Abraham) taught me this important wealth principle:

"All You Have to Do to Make a Fortune is Discover a Group of People Who are Already Getting Rich in Spite of Making Some Really Stupid Mistakes."

That's how we developed our Easy Passive Income System...

STEP ONE: I spent several years studying the individuals and companies who are making huge sums of money in the fundraising industry.

STEP TWO: My staff and I discovered what these people were doing to make huge sums of money. We found out what they were doing right and wrong.

STEP THREE: Then, we simply developed a powerful marketing system around fixing the 2 biggest mistakes that all of the successful people were making.

This is so great, I must say it again...

The marketing system we have developed for the Easy Passive Income System was built around the biggest mistakes that other people who are already making huge sums of money are making. As you will see, we have eliminated each mistake in a very powerful way.

Here are the 2 MAJOR MISTAKES...

MISTAKE #1: All the people who are making huge sums of money in the fundraising industry are following the follower. It's the blind leading the blind.

Tens of millions of people belong to some kind of group that needs to raise money for all of their activities. All you have to do is figure out an exciting new way to help them get what they want and you can become financially set for life.

It sounds simple. And it really can be.

After all, the world's greatest success coach – Zig Ziglar – said: "You can have anything you want if you will only help enough other people get what they want."

Zig was right.

My company has brought in tens of millions of dollars by doing everything possible to solve the biggest problems that large groups of people face. And the problems that we have solved with our Easy Passive Income System could potentially make you more money than you've ever dreamed possible. Read on...

THE PROBLEM:

Thousands of groups desperately need to raise money for all of their activities.

These groups depend on supporters to give them the money they need.

But many members HATE all of the things they have to constantly do to raise money. This is NOT the reason they joined the group and yet, they're FORCED to do it.

The fundraising programs never end. This month, they're selling candy bars, next month it's Christmas wrapping paper, and then the following month it might be some kind of raffle tickets to a charity event. Many of the group members HATE DOING THIS, and yet they must do it to be part of the group and to raise money for all of the activities.

The friends and family of these group members hate the fact that they are CONSTANTLY being hit up for money for stupid stuff they'd never buy otherwise.

Most people love to give, but hate the fact that they are constantly being asked to give more money... They have what fundraising industry insiders call DONOR BURNOUT.

The people who care the most and give

the most money are constantly being pressured to give more and more and more money. They begin to feel manipulated and taken advantage of.

The people who are already making a fortune in the fundraising industry have no real answer for all of the problems above.

And that's a big mistake...

You see, marketing is all about differentiation. It's setting yourself apart from the other companies who are doing everything they can to command the attention and interest of the same prospects you are trying to attract.

CONSIDER THIS: The people who make millions of dollars find ways to completely separate themselves from all the other companies in their marketplace. We spend a great deal of time and money to discover the weak points in our competitors' armor.

That sounds like a military metaphor, doesn't it? Well...

Marketing Can Be
a Lot Like Warfare.

Your competitors (with a few golden exceptions) are the enemy. These people are trying to take away the money that could and should be yours.

Does that sound ruthless? It's not, if what you're offering is truly legitimate in every way.

Listen closely. Many people make some very serious mistakes when it comes to the subject of competition. They either minimize it and pretend it doesn't exist, or blow it way out of proportion and become overly frightened and threatened by it.

You cannot make these mistakes. Do not turn a blind eye to the competition. They are out there trying to attract the same people you are trying to attract. Be aware of this, but...

Never Fear the Competition.

You can learn a lot by keeping your eyes wide open. Study the competition. Learn from them. Ask yourself, "What are they doing right and wrong?" And the most important question: "What can I do to completely separate myself from all of these other people?"

These are the questions we asked ourselves when we investigated all the people who are already making GIANT sums of money in the fundraising industry.

The answers to these questions became the solutions that you will now have when you do the one step that helps to introduce the group to our Passive Income Fundraising Program.

We have discovered a simple way to completely separate ourselves from all of the other individuals in the fundraising industry. This gives you a powerful advantage that none of these people have. You can use this advantage to make HUGE sums of money.

A moment ago, I summarized the huge problem that millions of people who belong to non-profit groups and their friends and family are going through. Now let me give you...

OUR SOLUTION

Our Passive Income Fundraising Program lets thousands of different groups raise the money they want and need without having to beg friends, family, and neighbors to buy something they don't even want!

Now these groups can do JUST ONE simple and easy fundraising program (by passing out an unlimited number of our free colorful DISCOUNT PRESCRIPTION CARDS or sending emails to people they know) and passively raise money that keeps coming in for many months and even years.

The friends and family members feel no pressure. The group members simply pass out the free cards to friends, family, and supporters of the group or get them to go to the group's website and instantly download their complementary DISCOUNT PRESCRIPTION CARD. This helps the cardholder get the absolute lowest prices on the prescriptions they need at over 54,000 pharmacies throughout the United States.

Everyone wins! The groups win, because they earn a passive income from a simple-to-use fundraising program that beats all the others. Their group can get a very nice check every single month, even if each group member passes out a small number of these cards. And their supporters win, because they get a super easy way to help the group raise money that doesn't cost them anything. In fact, it saves them money!

So remember the lesson I learned from the Jay Abraham. Jay is the world's most expensive marketing expert for a reason, he's a true master. And the important wealth principle he taught me can be worth huge sums of money to you.

Here's why: The people in the fundraising industry are making a lot of money in spite of the huge mistakes they continue to make. But we have solved those problems with our Easy Passive Income System. As you've seen, these people are simply "following the follower." There's nothing new and exciting about anything they're doing. The non-profit groups go along with the same old tired worn-out over-used fundraising programs they offer, because they don't have any other alternative... until now!

So think deeply about all of this. You'll see, this solves the first mistake that all of the people who are helping non-profit groups are making. Now let's move on to the next huge mistake we have solved...

MISTAKE #2: The people who are already making thousands of dollars a month are doing way too much personal selling.

Let me be very clear about the whole subject of personal selling: I hate it! And so do most of my friends and clients.

We hate the rejection. We are sick and tired of all the things that must be done to persuade other people to buy what we sell. We hate answering an endless series of objections. We hate intruding on other people.

THE BOTTOM LINE: All of us hate the pushiness of high-pressure selling. We hate the manipulation of aggressive salespeople who try to manipulate us into giving them our money. We hate being "sold."

Listen closely...

Personal Selling is the Most
Terrible Way to Make Money.

I did a lot of personal selling when I was younger, because I wanted to make good money and didn't have a college education. I've faced all the pain and humiliation of having hundreds of doors slammed in my face. I've had people hang up on me thousands of times. I've been yelled at and cursed at. I've faced all kinds of rejection.

I didn't know there was a better way...

HERE'S MY QUICK STORY: My friend, Ron Sheppeard, hired me as a salesperson in 1984. Before that, I was a welder in a factory. Ron knew I wanted more out of life and thought I'd make a good salesperson. He hired me, coached me, and gave me a lot of books to read and tapes to listen to.

It was a great, but painful education.

Becoming a salesperson led me to start my first business in December of 1985. I will always be grateful for that. But the only way I knew how to promote my company was to knock on doors and call people on the phone. Because of this, I've had thousands of doors slammed in my face and have been hung up on thousands of "cold calls." But I didn't know there was any better way to build my business...

Then in 1988 My Wife, Eileen, and I Discovered the Awesome Power of Direct Response Marketing and Our Lives Were Changed Forever.

This powerful form of marketing does all of the selling for you:

A. There is zero rejection.

B. You can sell to tens of thousands – and even millions – of people without talking to anyone.

C. The sales material and the methods you lump together into your marketing system do all the selling for you.

D. The only people you ever hear from are those who say "Yes!"

Direct Response Marketing is a little-known method that's responsible for over 300 billion dollars a year in total revenue. Yes, hundreds of billions are generated each year thanks to this powerful form of marketing. And yet, it remains virtually unknown to most business people and entrepreneurs...

So why don't more people know about this exciting wealth-making method? That's simple. You see, good Direct Response Marketing is what I call, "stealth marketing." It's like those fighter jets that remain undetected by radar. It's hard to spy on the people who are making millions in Direct Response and discover all of their hidden secrets.

This brings me to some good and bad news:

THE BAD NEWS:

Direct Response Marketing can be very

deceptive. On the surface, it seems so simple, and it really can be when you have all of the right elements in place... But underneath the surface there are many different strategies and methods that are responsible for the billions of dollars that are being generated each year. These more advanced methods remain hidden from the view of the novice who thinks or is led to believe that this is a simple and easy way to get rich.

THE GOOD NEWS:

We have taken all of the best-of-the-best of our Direct Response Marketing secrets that have brought us over $150-million dollars in less than 25 years and built them into our ONE STEP MARKETING SYSTEM that's designed to make you huge sums of money from the comfort of your own home.

Here are 5 MAIN REASONS why the one

step you'll be using to cash in with our Easy Passive Income System has the ability to make you tens of thousands of dollars a month:

1. It lets you tap into the awesome power of Direct Response Marketing.

2. It is based on proven methods that have made us tens of millions of dollars.

3. We have built it for you and can run most of your business for you. Yes, we can do almost everything for you. All you do is the one simple step, which involves mailing the materials we give you. This introduces the non-profit groups to our Passive Income Fundraising Program. That's it. Everything else is done for you by our company and our health technology partner who is making our Discount

Prescription Card Program available to the group.

4.   This is a truly duplicatable wealth-making system. It's the same system we're using to reach our goal of bringing in massive sums of money.

5.   It gives you an unfair advantage over all of the other people who are already making huge sums of money in the fundraising industry.

Remember, this Easy Passive Income System completely eliminates the major mistakes everyone else is making:

SOLUTION for MISTAKE #1:

It Does an Amazing Job of Separating You from All of the Other Competitors.

SOLUTION for MISTAKE #2:

It Does a Complete Job of Selling for You.
You Will Never Have to Talk with Anyone!

Our Easy Passive Income System is the most powerful way to cash in with Direct Response Marketing because the amount of money you can quickly generate from each group who gets involved in our fundraising program can easily cover your marketing costs.

This lets you tap into the tremendous power of 2-step marketing...

STEP ONE: It attracts the highest quality prospects only and repels all others.

STEP TWO: It sells the largest percentage of these prospects for the maximum profit possible.

Our Easy Passive Income System Gives You
the Ultimate Way to Let Up to Hundreds –
or Perhaps Thousands – of Other
People Make Money for You.

When you completely understand
everything that has gone into this powerful
system, you will be speechless!

And when you add all 5 of the reasons I just
gave you together – they all boil down to one
major advantage:

They Give You the Same Benefits
the World's Richest People Enjoy.

CONSIDER THIS: The world's richest people
make money on many things that have nothing to
do with the amount of time and work they actually
do. They make money from the efforts of other
people, from the sale of certain products or

services, or from other income producing assets that let them sit back and let other things make more money for them.

Yes, these wealthy people have many ways to continue to earn a fortune, even when they do nothing. Now you can enjoy these same powerful advantages.

And that brings me to an important point I told you about in the Introduction.

It's the fact that there are only 3 ways to make money.

Here they are again:

MONEY-MAKING METHOD #1:

You Can Sell Your Time for Money.

This is the way 99% of the people make

almost all of their money. Everyone from day laborers who slave under the hot sun for minimum wage, to brain surgeons who get paid thousands of dollars an hour. All of these people are selling their time for money.

MONEY-MAKING METHOD #2:

You Can Sell a Product or Service
or Combination of Both.

With this second method, your money comes from the sale of some product or service, not the amount of time you work. This is a much smarter way to make money. In fact, the world is filled with many millionaires who make almost all of their money with this second powerful method.

But the real secret to getting rich is to use the final method.

Just look...

MONEY-MAKING METHOD #3:

Passive Income! You Use Your Money
to Make You Even More Money.

The 2nd method is quite capable of making you very rich. But the third method of making money has made more people wealthy than the other two combined. With this final method, you are putting your money into income-producing assets that automatically make you more money... All you do is sit back and cash the checks you receive for all of your investments.

And now for the best news:

Our Easy Passive Income System is one of the most powerful ways to make money in the entire world, because ALL the money you can make will come from the 2nd and 3rd methods which are responsible for the GIANT fortunes of the world's richest people.

The Amount of Money You Can Earn
Has Nothing to Do with the Amount
of Actual Time and Work You Put in.

And this leads to the biggest benefit of all...

Because After You Do the One Step
(Which Introduces Our Fundraising Program
to the Non-Profit Groups) Our Company
and Our Health Technology Partner
Will Do All of the Work for You and –
Because of That – It is Possible for You
to Make Many Thousands of Dollars
a Month Without Doing Any Work.

Of course, there are no promises and
guarantees that you will make up to $100,000 a
year or any specific sum of money for doing
absolutely no work – but the potential to get paid
many thousands of dollars for letting us run

everything for you is definitely here.

Here's why:

Your income comes from the sale of the fundraising program. And as you've seen, just a small number of groups who use our program could add up to a huge monthly income for you.

The sales material, our proven methods, and our expertly trained staff do all the selling for you.

And you also have the amazing opportunity to get paid from as many as hundreds or even thousands of other people who are using our DISCOUNT PRESCRIPTION CARDS to save up to 87% on all of their prescription medications.

The more you understand this – the more thrilled you will be.

But for now, let me end this book, by telling

you more about the powerful marketing method that is the foundation behind our Easy Passive Income System.

I want to help you understand more about the exciting Direct-Response Marketing methods that have been built into this powerful system. Only then will you truly know that this simple System really can make you financially set for life. So go to the next chapter now! As you're about to see, this gives you the ability to make more money than you ever dreamed possible. Please read carefully. By the time you're done with this book, you may be so excited you'll need a pill to get to sleep tonight!

CHAPTER NINE

The Awesome Power of Direct Response Marketing and Why It Can Quickly Make You the Fortune You Deserve.

Direct Response Marketing is the secret behind our Easy Passive Income System. This makes it easy for you to do one simple step that takes as little as 10-minutes a day and put yourself in position to earn more money than most people make working full time. That may have sounded too good to be true when you started this book, but by now, you are hopefully beginning to realize that it is true!

This form of marketing is the world's greatest way to make money. So I thought I'd devote an entire chapter to helping you understand it. As I told you in the last chapter, this little-known method made my wife, Eileen, and me over ten million dollars in our first five years. We started with only a few hundred dollars back in 1988, and when the smoke cleared a few years later, we were millionaires.

The same thing can happen to you.

This is a method of marketing that can make you more money in a faster period of time, than any other method. It has been responsible for many rags-to-riches success stories like ours. It has the power to make you a multi-millionaire in just a few short years from today.

Yes, think about that:

In Just a Few Years from the Time
You are Reading This Book –
You Could Make Millions of Dollars.

Please keep that thought as we continue...

But wait. Maybe you're asking yourself, "If this is a method that's making many people like you and your wife instant millionaires, why do you say it is a "little-known" method?"

That's a great question!

The answer is simple: You see, many people are interested in getting rich in Direct Response Marketing. This is one of the most exciting ways to make money. And many people fall in love with the idea of getting rich with this powerful form of marketing.

But as I told you in the last chapter, this method of marketing is deceptive.

You see, on the surface it sounds simple, and when you have all the elements working together in the right way, it really is. However, there are many different details that must be understood and mastered if you want to make millions of dollars in the shortest period of time. Many people don't want to put in the time and work to study and master the more advanced features of Direct Response Marketing. They go into this half-cocked and do not experience the results they want. Then they quit, and move onto something else.

I'll go into a few of the complexities of this powerful wealth-building method in a moment.

And if you pay close attention, and spend some time understanding these challenges and face them head-on, you really could become a millionaire in no time flat.

But first, let's talk about the good things...

Here's the 5 main reasons why this method of marketing can put millions of dollars in your bank account in a few short years:

1. This proven method is responsible for well over one billion dollars in sales each day.

2. This powerful method of marketing lets you sell to millions of people with no rejection.

3. There is little or even no risk, if you do it right.

4.   You can make millions of dollars from the comfort and privacy of your home.

5.   When done correctly, a good Direct Response Marketing System is less like a business, and more similar to a well-oiled money machine.

Let's go over each one of these reasons why this can make you the fast fortune you seek...

REASON #1: This is a proven method that's responsible for well over one billion dollars a day.

The Direct Response Marketing Association says that over 300 billion dollars are being generated each year through this powerful marketing method. Personally, I believe they are being way too conservative. I believe the "real" number is over twice that amount.

But what difference does it make if it's one

or two billion dollars a day? The point is: This proven wealth-making method is making a fortune for tens of thousands of individuals and companies right now. It's like a giant safe that's filled with millions of dollars... All you gotta do is know the combination on the lock and all the money inside is yours.

Now listen carefully. Many people want to make millions of dollars in the fastest time, and that's great... But these people never stop to realize that all the money they want to make is out there right now. This is true for you, too.

Yes, All the Money
You Want to Make is
Waiting for You Right Now!

Where is this money?

That's simple: It's in the pockets, purses, and

bank accounts and credit card limits of tens of millions of people. All you have to do is use the power of Direct Response Marketing to offer them something that's worth far more money than the sum you are asking for, and they will gladly give this money to you.

This is great news for you!

Why?

Because our powerful marketing system is designed to give hundreds of millions of people something that is far more valuable that what you're asking them to do in return.

By the time you have read and studied all the materials we have developed for you (in our Easy Passive Income System, you'll know exactly why this simple system has the awesome potential to make you a millionaire in no time flat.

REASON #2: You can sell to millions of people with ZERO rejection.

The people who make millions of dollars in Direct Response Marketing think of it as a method for selling. This is the right way to think of this...

It's Not Advertising.
It's Not Marketing.
It is Selling.

When you think of Direct Response from this perspective, you will be light years ahead of all the other people who try this money-making method and fail.

So why is this way of thinking so important?

Simple:

It Lets You Develop the
Right Strategies and Methods
That Can Make You Rich.

When you think of Direct Response Marketing as a powerful form of selling, you will automatically develop the right strategies that can make you more money than you have ever dreamed possible.

So what is sel ing? Here is my definition:

1.   Selling is serving.

2.   It is finding out what people want more than anything else, and discovering a way to give it to them.

3.   It is all the things you do to attract the type of people who are perfect for what you offer and repel the wrong ones.

4.   It is everything you do to educate, persuade, and influence people to buy from you, and keep buying.

5.   It is all you do to prove that what you have to offer is worth far more than the money you're asking for in return.

6.   It is about building a strong case of all the reasons why it is in your prospects best interest to give you their money in exchange for what the items you are offering.

7.   It's all the things you do to make people feel good about their decision to give you their hard-earned money.

When the process of selling is done correctly, people will know they made the right decision because you did a great job of educating them on all of the benefits of your products or services. They will be convinced they made a great decision to do business with you. You will have earned their business because you helped them get something they really wanted.

When Done Correctly, a Good Direct Response Marketing Campaign Will Replace a Live Salesperson. In fact, the Sales Materials and Systems You Develop are Better Than Any Salesperson You Could Ever Hire.

There are a lot of great salespeople, but no matter how good they are, all people make mistakes. We have good days and bad days. We have times when we're on top of our game and off days when nothing goes right. We get sick... We have problems... We are easily distracted by an endless number of problems, challenges, and situations. And when you hire salespeople to work for you, there will be days when they do a good job and sell lots of products and services, and other days when they can't give them away.

But a good Direct Response Marketing campaign does not have these problems.

When done correctly, a great salesperson will build the Direct Response Marketing campaign from the ground up to do a powerful job of selling. They will use their experience and knowledge to build a solid case for the product or service being sold. They will pour their heart and soul into the sales materials. All of their energy and passion and excitement for the items being sold will go into these materials and the well-thought-out sequence and methods that will sell the products and services to the largest percentage of prospective buyers.

In other words – when done correctly – Direct Response Marketing is a powerful way

to duplicate the highly skilled work of
the very best professional salesperson:

√   It does a complete job of selling.

√   It never gets tired or has an off day.

√   It never calls in sick.

√   It is never distracted by all the
challenges of life.

THE BOTTOM LINE: Most people fail in Direct Response Marketing because they do not understand that the true purpose of a Direct Response Marketing campaign is to fully replace a live salesperson.

Does this sound too simple?

It's not. In fact, this is one of the main

secrets that made us tens of millions of dollars. Best of all, it's the secret we have built into our Easy Passive Income System.

Our powerful system does a complete job of selling for you. It's like hiring the very best salesperson in the world who will go to work for you 24 hours a day, to make you the largest sum of money.

The step you do introduces the non-profit groups to our revolutionary fundraising program. From that point forward, we do everything else. We do all we can to sign the groups up on your behalf and help them raise all the money they want and need. As you've seen, this can pay you an ongoing passive monthly income that can keep growing bigger.

REASON #3: When you do this correctly – there is no risk.

Okay – here's where things really heat up...

In a moment, I'm going to tell you about a few of the main problems with Direct Response Marketing. This really is the world's greatest way to get rich, but there are some pitfalls to avoid. Once you know what they are, you can make a GIANT fortune, just as I have.

But for now, let me give you the BIGGEST problem with Direct Response Marketing:

The High Cost.

As I have proven to you, this is a very powerful form of selling. In fact, having hard-hitting 1,000 Direct Mail sales letters in the mail is similar to having 1,000 of the best salespeople in the world who make money for you night and day.

But its strength is also its weakness.

Why do I say this?

That's simple.

You see, to do it right, a good Direct Response Marketing campaign can be very expensive. Many people don't factor in these high costs and end up failing.

But the solution is rather simple:

Just sell high-ticket items that people desperately want, with a huge perceived value and a large margin of profit.

That's it. This is all you do to put yourself in the powerful position to get very rich. It sounds simple, because it is.

You see, most people never get rich in Direct Response Marketing because they simply choose the wrong products or services to sell. They set themselves up to fail because the items they offer have these basic problems:

1. There is no "real" demand for the items being sold. In other words, most people don't want them.

2. The items do not sell for enough money to cover the high cost of the Direct Response Marketing campaign.

Because our Easy Passive Income System eliminates BOTH of these major problems. The sales materials we'll give you is designed to reach non-profit groups. And as you've seen, all it takes are a small number of groups who use our revolutionary fundraising program to make you huge sums of money. As an example only: if the materials you'll be sending out ultimately helps us introduce our program to just 20 groups of 150 members each, who used the methods we give them to pass out our free DISCOUNT PRESCRIPTION CARDS to 10 of their friends and family members and if these people used our savings card to fill an average of 1 prescription a month, you would get paid $10,500 a month.

That's $126,000 a Year in Passive Income.

Remember, that's potential, not promised income. Nobody can ethically and legally promise that you will get paid as much as $126,00 a year or any specific amount, and that's not what I'm doing with these examples.

However, the examples in this book are your proof that you really could potentially get paid a six figure annual income from just a small number of non-profit groups who are introduced to our Passive Income Fundraising Program, thanks to the one step that you do. Isn't that exciting? Say "YES!" And this solves the major problem of the high cost of Direct Response Marketing.

That leads us to the next major advantage...

REASON #4: You can make money from the comfort and privacy of your own home.

Yes, it's amazing – but true. My wife and I started with only $300.00 and turned it into over $10,000,000 in our first five years. Who knows, you may do even better!

I can't promise that you will make hundreds of thousands or millions of dollars in a few short years like we did. But I can promise and guarantee that it is possible to get very rich. In fact, there are many Direct-Response Marketing multi-millionaires who make our rags-to-riches success story seem pale by comparison.

In fact:

This is a Method of Marketing That Can
Easily Make You More Money Than Almost
All of the Richest People in Your Area.

Consider this:

√ You can make money without leaving your home.

√ You can make sales without talking to anyone.

√ You can get off to a very powerful start for a very low amount of money.

√ And thanks to our Easy Passive Income System, once you do the one step, which introduces the non-profit groups to our amazing fundraising program, everything else is done for you!

So add it up. You'll see. These main benefits all lead to the final major advantage of a good Direct Response Marketing campaign...

REASON #5: A good Direct Response

MAKE MONEY HELPING PEOPLE

Marketing campaign is similar to having a money machine that cranks out thousands of dollars a day.

Imagine how it would be to own a money-making machine. All you'd have to do is press a few buttons and thousands of dollars would come pouring out.

Whatever amount of money you want can be yours by simply turning a few knobs:

√   Need $500 a day? Great. Just run your machine for a little longer and it's yours.

√   Need $1,000 a day? That's okay, too. Just turn on your machine and come back later. The money will be waiting for you.

Does this sound exciting to you?

Would you like to have your own powerful money machine if it really was possible?

Of course you would.

But all this sounds like a great fantasy, doesn't it?

Well, in some ways it is, and in other ways it's not.

You See, When You Get All the Elements Working Together in Just the Right Way...

A Good Direct Response Marketing Campaign is Similar to Owning a Money Machine That Can Make Giant Sums of Money for You.

How much money?

Well, let me put it this way...

I have had days where my small company – in the tiny town of Goessel, Kansas – has brought in over...

$100,000 a Day.

Yes, here we are, a small company in the middle of nowhere (I challenge you to find Goessel, Kansas on a map) and there have been days we made over $100,000.

Now wait a minute, I'm not telling you about all the times we made over $100,000 a day to brag.

No way!

I hate it when people who show off. I'm sure you feel the same way. The only reason I tell you about the days we used our Direct Response Marketing secrets to bring in over $100,000 a day is because: I firmly believe that if we can use these amazing secrets to bring in over one hundred thousand dollars a day, then you can use them to bring in over $100,000 a year or much more.

> This is Especially True When You consider Everything That We are Offering to Give You When You Become Involved with Us in Our Easy Passive Income System.

The above statement (and everything else in this book) is only my opinion. But as you can see, it's based on solid fact. This is especially true when you stop and realize that our Easy Passive Income System contains all of the greatest tips, tricks, strategies, and basic materials and methods that have brought my very small company (headquartered in a very small town in Kansas) over...

$150,000,000 in Less Than 25 years.

Yes, as you know, my wife, Eileen, and I

began in September of 1988 with only a few hundred dollars and parlayed it into over a grand total of $10-million dollars in our first 5 years.

We could have sat back and retired, but we didn't.

Instead, we fe l in love with Direct Response Marketing and have been on a mission (Yes, that sounds corny, but it's true.) to help other average people make money with our best secrets.

We have seen and studied thousands of different opportunities since 1988... But our Easy Passive Income System is our greatest discovery ever. This lets you tap into the full power of all of the greatest secrets we have used to generate tens of millions of dollars in Direct Response Marketing. There are no guarantees that you will make any specific sum of money, but I am living proof that it's more than possible. And many multi-millionaires make our story pale by comparison.

When you add up everything we've talked about – you can see why I firmly believe that this powerful marketing method can make you all the money you want from the comfort and privacy of your home.

But no subject on getting rich with this powerful marketing method would be complete without covering a few of the major pitfalls of this powerful wealth-making method. I have shown you the top reasons why this really can make you a fortune in a few short years, starting with very little money.

Now let me show you why most people never get rich with this world's greatest wealth-making method...

Here are 3 main reasons why most people

never make millions of dollars with Direct
Response Marketing:

1. They don't factor in the high costs.

2. They choose the wrong products or
services to sell.

3. They never master the complexities of
this marketing method.

So let's go over each one and I'll tell you
how our Easy Passive Income System solves each
problem for you:

Direct-Response Marketing Problem #1:

Most People Never Factor in the High Costs
of This Powerful Marketing Method.

Direct Response is the most powerful

marketing method in the world, but it's also the second most expensive method of selling. (The most expensive method is to hire a sales representative to personally call on prospects and customers.) Most newcomers don't factor in these high costs. And most promoters who offer Direct Response opportunities do not educate you on the high costs.

The bottom line: Everyone wants to bury their heads in the sand on this issue. I have in the past... And I see many others making this terrible mistake.

Here's how I made this mistake: For years I have been obsessed with finding a way to mix multi-level or network marketing with Direct Response Marketing. I tried many things and spent hundreds of thousands of dollars. It was like beating my head against the wall. I kept running into problem after problem that could not be solved. Sure, I had some successes. But the #1 problem keeps staring me in the face:

With Most MLM Opportunities – There is Not Enough Profit on the Initial Sale to Absorb the High Costs of Making That Sale.

There is not enough money left over after all the marketing is done to cover all of my costs.

And that brings us to the next item...

Direct-Response Marketing Problem #2:

Most Newcomers to Direct Response Marketing Choose the Wrong Products or Services to Sell.

Some experts say that "anything can be sold by mail." I've probably heard this a thousand times. My response is, "Maybe."

You see, I firmly believe that we are only limited by our imaginations and willingness to do whatever it takes. So I think they are right. But just because you can do something doesn't mean you should do it.

The truth is, some products and services are perfect for Direct Response Marketing and others are not. So why work harder than you have to? Why make it more difficult than it has to be?

Why not use this simple formula instead: Find the types of items that sell like hotcakes for other people via Direct Response Marketing and only say "Yes!" to promoting these types of products and services and say "No." to everything else. It's a simple formula, but most people will never use it.

Don't make this mistake. You must only fall in love with the most profitable items the people in some lucrative market want the most. Just run every new idea through a screen to see if other people are already getting rich with similar items... If not, avoid the product or service like the plague.

This one simple idea has brought us tens of millions of dollars.

Here's how you can use this idea:

1.   Choose markets that are already making many money for people.

2.   Find products and services with tremendous perceived value and super-high profit margins.

3.   Make sure you have a complete strategy n place to make a nice profit

even if everything goes wrong and your overall response rates are very low.

If you can do these simple things the right way, you can make huge sums of money, just as we have. And that's good news for you because...

Our Easy Passive Income System Was Built Around This Very Simple Wealth-Making Formula.

This is the ultimate discovery we have ever made for completely eliminating the first two problems that stop most people from getting rich in Direct Response Marketing.

Now let's go to the last major problem...

Direct-Response Marketing Problem #3:

Most People Never Master the Complexities of This Powerful Marketing Method.

One of the smartest marketing experts I know says: "Marketing takes a day to learn and a lifetime to master." He's right. On the surface, there is nothing as simple as Direct Response Marketing. After all, this can be as easy as running some ads or mailing postcards and sending out a sales letter to all the people who request more information. What could be simpler than that?

But remember, Direct Response Marketing is misleading... You see, underneath the surface, this is a method of marketing that can take many years to master.

This Wealth-Making Method
is Like a Game of Chess.

To the person who is new to this game, it all looks very simple. After all, there are only six different pieces on a board with some red and black squares. How hard could that be? Right?

Well, as you know, it can be very difficult. In fact you can spend your whole life trying to understand all of the complexities of this wonderful game. Many do. And only a few of the world's greatest chess masters have ever been able to beat a chess software program that runs on a small laptop computer. You see, within those six individual pieces on those red and black squares, there are millions of different moves that can be made.

Direct Response Marketing is just like this...

In fact:

This is the Ultimate Wealth-Making
Game You Can Play and Win Big!

The people who make millions of dollars with

this marketing method every year have usually been at it for a number of years. My wife and I did make over ten million dollars in our first four years, but we are an exception to the rule. And besides, our own success was due in large part to the expert help we received from people like Russ von Hoelscher, Jay Abraham, Jeff Gardner, Brad and Alan Antin, Chris Lakey, Drew Hansen, Dan Kennedy, and Eric J. Bechtold, and our willingness to do whatever these experts told us to do.

Now think about this:

Many People Get into Direct Response Marketing Because They Believe It's a Simple and Easy Way to Get Rich. This Attracts Lazy and Delusional People Like a Magnet is Attracted to Steel.

These lazy people see how simple this powerful form of marketing is on the surface, jump in with both feet, experience early defeat, and then quit as fast as they started. They go through a few hard times and now they're on to the next opportunity that promises fast and easy overnight riches.

But the people who make millions of dollars are different.

Those of us who have made a fortune know that this form of marketing can be complicated and difficult. But we didn't let these obstacles as challenges stop us. We kept going through all of the difficulties until we mastered the more advanced methods.

These self-made millionaires (of which I am a proud member) are earning the rewards for not giving up. We have paid the price by spending many years to discover solutions to all of the problems that stop the beginner. Now we're sitting back and making huge sums of money with relative ease.

This Same Powerful Wealth-Making Advantage Can Now Be Yours.

But what if you don't have ten years to master these little-known tips, tricks, and strategies? What if you're willing to do whatever it takes, but you want to get rich in the fastest time possible?

What then?

Well, in most cases, you are out of luck. Sure, there are many different Direct Response Marketing opportunities to choose from. But most of them will never make you a fast fortune.

The reason is simple: Most of these programs are designed to make the promoters rich. These people give you a product to sell and some sales material to sell it (usually on a website) and now they want you to believe their "turn-key package" can make you rich.

But have they used this sales material themselves? Has it been tested and proven to bring in massive sums of money? Most times the answer is "No!" And do these promoters make their largest profits by helping you get rich? Again, the answer is "No!" Almost all of their money comes from the sale of their pre-packaged opportunity. After that, they have no real incentive to help you make money.

But This is One More Area Where
Our Easy Passive Income System Beats
All of Those Other Programs Combined.

Remember, our largest profits come from helping you make money with all of the materials and methods in our Easy Passive Income System. In fact, all you do is one simple step and we take care of everything else for you.

I realize that all this sounded too good to be true when you first picked up this book, but, by now, you hopefully realize that it is true.

Remember, as an example only, if you had just 20 groups of 150 members each, who passed our free DISCOUNT PRESCRIPTION CARDS to 10 of their friends and family members and when these people used our savings card to fill an average of 1 prescription a month, you just got paid $10,500 a month, or $126,000 a year in totally passive in.

So please think deeply about how much good our Easy Passive Income System does for so many people. Then create your own mathematical charts and consider how much money you could potentially make for various numbers of groups who are using our DISCOUNT PRESCRIPTION CARDS to raise the money they need. Do this and you'll see, the potential to get paid huge sums of money is definitely here. We can't promise that you'll get paid as much as $126,000 a year or any specific amount and are not showing you these examples as a promise that you will make any specific amount of money. The amount of commissions you get paid will be based on the number of your non-profit groups that we will be working with (for you), how many savings cards they pass out, and how many people use the cards when they fill their prescriptions. Your results will vary based on many factors, and we can't guarantee you'll make any specific sum of money. However, it's important to remember that the more money we can put in your bank account, the more we deposit into our own. This gives us the greatest reason to do all we can to see to it that you get paid the largest amount of money for the longest period of time.

Listen closely. I have always loved to help other people make huge sums of money. In fact, my friends make fun of me and tell me I should have gone into the ministry. Perhaps they're right. But I don't care. The fact is: I remember all the pain that my wife and I had to go through to learn how to get rich, and anything I can do to help other people who have similar dreams of getting rich is one of the greatest things I can do.

But I'm only human. And even though I love helping other people get rich, there's one thing I enjoy even more... I love any opportunity that lets me make a fortune by helping other people fill up their bank accounts.

Many opportunities promise to let you make money by helping others. After all, isn't this what multi-level or network marketing is all about? But as you may know, very few live up to their claims.

But Our PASSIVE INCOME Program
Lives Up to All Its Claims.

In all my years of researching thousands of different opportunities, I have never seen such a powerful way to make easy money. There is so much for you to keep in mind about this powerful home business. But the most important thing is the fact that my company can make a nice ongoing profit for all of the money we can make for you.

This Gives Us the Most Powerful Reason
to Do Everything Within Our Power
to See to It That You Get Paid Up to
Thousands of Dollars Every Month.

We have taken the best of all the methods

and materials that have brought us tens of millions of dollars and boiled them down into a simple system that gives us the potential to make big profits by doing everything we can to help you make the most money possible.

Yes, All of the Greatest Secrets We Have Discovered Since 1988 Have Gone into This Powerful and Proven Easy Passive Income System.

In all my years as a professional business opportunity researcher, I have never seen a more powerful way that I can personally make all the money you want and need by doing all I can to help YOU make huge sums of automatic money.

My staff and I have spent hundreds of hours, boiling down our greatest secrets into a simple system that gives you the power to get rich by doing one simple and easy (but very important) step. We have spent many years mastering all of the complexities of Direct Response Marketing, so you don't have to. And it really is in our best interest to do everything we can to help you deposit huge sums of money into your personal bank account.

The more you know about this powerful home business opportunity, the more excited you'll be.

But now it's time to move on... In the next chapter, I will give you a complete summary of our Easy Passive Income System and shows you how to get started right away. Read on...

SECTION THREE

Getting
Started.

CHAPTER TEN

Conclusion.

Congratulations for having officially read "Make Money Helping People" from beginning to end. I hope you're excited about this opportunity!

If you've gone through this book, you know that our Easy Passive Income System can make you all the money you've ever wanted.

- You can make money from the comfort and privacy of your home.

- You can make big money in as little as 10-minutes a day.

- You can get paid a pure passive income... for life!

- You could potentially get paid up to $875 a month – to $5,250 – to as much as $10,500 a month or more, for letting our system help the groups who need to raise money.

This is completely moral – ethical – and even fun! Plus, this gives you the same type of benefits of a very expensive franchise that costs as much as $50,000 to $100,000 or more. This chapter gives you a summary of the main things that make this opportunity so special. I'll cover all of them. Then I'll tell you how to get started.

For starters, there has never been a way to make up to thousands of dollars a month, while also helping so many others at the same time... until now!

THE PROBLEM:

Americans pay some of the highest retail costs for prescription drugs in the world. And even for those who have insurance, the deductibles and co-pays put even necessary drugs out of reach for many families, forcing them to choose between medicine or food. For these families on the fringe, the ability to have one more option that can save them money is a lifesaver.

OUR SOLUTION:

Through a partnership with a major national health technology company, our absolutely free DISCOUNT PRESCRIPTION CARD helps people save money by solving the terrible problem of runaway drug costs. At the time of this writing, our discount prescription cardholders have already saved $179,109,815 off the regular prices of the prescription drugs they need. And those savings increase every single day!

There is a huge and growing need to save up to 87% on all prescription medications – and we have discovered an easy way that YOU can cash-in from the huge demand.

Our core system allows Affiliates to make passive cash by using our easy methods to get our discount drug cards into the hands of the people who desperately need to save money on their prescription medications.

As an affiliate, you can get paid a passive residual income on every prescription filled, when our card was used to get the discount.

Plus, you continue to make money as families go back to the pharmacy for refills and new prescriptions. In fact, once our card is used, it usually stays in the pharmacy's records system, so you can continue to get credit for prescriptions each time they are filled and refilled, month after month.

BUT WAIT... That's only the start of how you make money.

Because Our Easy Passive Income
System Lets You Make Even More Money
by Tapping into a Massive Source of
People Who are Eager to Do All of the
Work for You to Get These Discount
Cards into the Hands of Hundreds
or Thousands of Others...

These people are members of churches or other non-profit groups who need to raise money for all of their various activities.

Our system is designed to let you make money by introducing our program to these non-profit groups. You do one step. We do the rest.

As you've seen, this lets the groups raise the funds they need, while paying you an automatic residual income on all the "work" they do. This has the power to give you complete financial security for life, while doing SO MUCH GOOD for so many others.

We call our program the "Passive Income Fundraising Program."

There are 3 basic components:

1. Helping groups raise money without the headaches and hassles that most fundraisers require...

2. Helping people save money on their prescription medications...

3. And paying YOU passive income!

As you've seen, this is...

The ULTIMATE
SOLUTION

Here's why: All honest and legitimate opportunities solve some kind of major problems for as many people as possible. There is no other way to become financially independent.

Just find millions of people with HUGE PROBLEMS. Then discover or develop a product or service that solves these problems in the BIGGEST WAY. That's it. That's all there is to it. If you can solve a big enough problem for enough people, then you can make a lot of money and enjoy complete and total financial security. This is what you can have when you get involved in this amazing opportunity.

PROBLEM #1:

Millions of people are paying too much for

their prescription drugs. OUR SOLUTION: Our DISCOUNT PRESCRIPTION CARD lets people save up to 87% off on each FDA approved drug at over 54,000 pharmacies nationwide.

PROBLEM #2:

Thousands of groups desperately need to raise money for all of their activities. OUR SOLUTION: Our Passive Income Fundraising Program lets these groups raise the money they need without having to beg friends, family, and neighbors to buy something they don't even want!

PROBLEM #3:

The friends and family of these group members hate the fact that they are constantly being asked to give more money for things they'd never buy otherwise. OUR SOLUTION: The supporters use their free DISCOUNT

PRESCRIPTION CARD to save up to 87% on the prescription drugs they're already taking. This gives them an easy way to help the group raise money, without spending a single dollar. They save money on the medications they need and help the group raise money. Brilliant!

PROBLEM #4:

Many people need a way to make more money, without all of the headaches and hassles. They desperately want to make money with NO long hours, NO large start-up cost and NO personal selling. OUR SOLUTION: As an Affiliate of our Easy Passive Income System, you will use our complete system that lets you make money by helping us introduce our revolutionary program to the groups who desperately need a simple and easy way to raise money. You'll do everything from the comfort and privacy of your own home. This gives you a complete way to get paid a passive monthly income in just minutes a day.

Add it up. You'll see...

EVERYONE WINS!

√ The group wins, because they get an easy and automatic way to raise all of the money they need for their group activities.

√ Their supporters win, because they save a lot of money on their prescription medications and help the group raise money.

√ And YOU WIN, because you can get started for a super low fee and then let our automated system do everything for you. As you'll see, this gives you the most powerful way to achieve complete and total financial security ... and hardly lift a finger.

HOW YOU MAKE MONEY:

You will use our 20-Second System to process mail that introduces our exciting and proven Passive Income Fundraising Program to the groups. Each group is issued a special fundraising code and an initial batch of 5,000 DISCOUNT PRESCRIPTION CARDS they can give away for free. Then every prescription that's filled with this code is credited to you and the group. They receive $1.50 every time each one of their friends and family members use our savings cards, and you earn 35 cents. As you've seen, this small amount can add up to huge profits for you!

It's so simple. It's so brilliant. The groups pass out their DISCOUNT PRESCRIPTION CARDS to their friends and family, along with a special letter that tells them about our unique fundraising program and makes them want to participate. Each time they use the groups card to fill an authorized prescription, the group gets paid, and so do you!

How Much Could You Make?

The amount of commissions you can get is based on the number of your groups that we will be working with [for you], how many savings cards they pass out, and how many people use the cards to fill their prescriptions. Your results will vary based on many factors, so we can't guarantee you'll make any specific sum. But it is possible to make $100,000 a year or more, by using our 20-second system to process mail that introduces our Passive Income Fundraising Program to the non-profit groups and letting them and us do the rest. You can count on us to do all we can to help you make the largest amount of money, because the more you make, the more we make.

So with all that said, let me remind you the examples I gave you in this book. Remember, these are based on mathematical projections only, but they do a great job of showing you how much money you could potentially make:

EXAMPLE #1:

If you were to use our Easy Passive Income System to sign up only 10 groups who each had 25 members who passed out 10 DISCOUNT PRESCRIPTION CARDS to their friends and family members, and each cardholder fills an average of 1 prescription a month, the groups would get $3,750 a month. That's great news for them! After all, they just raised $3,750 a month and they never had to go through all of the headaches and hassles of most fundraising programs. But it's even better for YOU, because in this example, you would also get your own monthly check for $875.

EXAMPLE #2:

If you had just 10 groups of 150 members each, who passed our free DISCOUNT PRESCRIPTION CARDS to an average of 10 of their friends and family members, and when these people used our savings card to fill an average of 1 prescription a month, you would get paid $5,250 a month. That's $63,000 a year!

EXAMPLE #3:

And if you had just 20 groups of 150 members each, who passed our free DISCOUNT PRESCRIPTION CARDS to 10 of their friends and family members and if these people used our savings card to fill an average of 1 prescription a month, you'd get paid $10,500 a month in totally passive income!

Those are examples only. I can't promise that you'll get up to $126,000 a year or any specific amount. Your groups could pass out even more DISCOUNT PRESCRIPTION CARDS or have a higher-than-average number of prescriptions filled each month. But as all three of these mathematical examples prove, the potential to get paid as much as $875 to $10,500 a month in passive income or more is here!

But having said all that, you also know:

✔ This lets you make money and rewards you for helping so many other people.

✔ No other home-based business lets you make so much money and do so much good for so many people.

✔ This is completely moral – ethical –

and even fun! Plus, this gives you all of the same type of benefits of a very expensive franchise that costs as much as $50,0C0 to $100,000 or more.

✔   And finally: This is totally private. You will never have to talk with anyone (unless you want to). Our company, the DISCOUNT PRESCRIPTION CARD company – and the groups do all of the work for you.

And when you add it all up, you'll realize that, as hard as it may to have believed in the beginning, this really does give you...

The Power to Stay Home Each Day
and Get a Huge Passive Income.

This opportunity lets you get paid on the efforts of many other people. It's the same advantage the most successful people have, and now it's yours for a very low one-time fee.

How it works:

A.   Just fill out the form on the last page
of this book and mail or fax it to me.
My staff and I will send you complete
information about how to become a
Representative for our Easy Passive
Income System.

B.   Just cover the one-time fee to become
a Representative and I will enroll you
as an Affiliate for the health
technology company who is providing
the Prescription Savings Cards. This
company is the foundation of our Easy
Passive Income System. The low price
to become an affiliate for their
company will include 5,000 of your
own Discount Prescription Cards.

C.   I'll have our health technology partner send your custom-printed Prescription Savings Cards to you. Then I'll rush you my complete Easy Passive Income System. This lets you cash-in with everything you've read about in this book.

THIS IS ONLY FOR YOU.

None of the other Affiliates who are already making money with these Discount Prescription Cards have all of the secrets and turn-key materials you will receive when you become a Representative of our Easy Passive Income System. This could potentially pay you as much as $10,500 a month for only minutes a day. That's potential, not promised income. But – if you've read everything in this book you know – this amazing home business opportunity truly does have the power to pay you huge sums of passive income!

But you must hurry. I can only work with so many people. **The materials you'll be using to introduce the groups to our Fundraising Program all have my personal phone number on them.** My staff and I can only work with so many non-profit groups on a daily basis. Therefore, I'll have to cancel this opportunity whenever I feel we're working with too many groups. If you put this off and fill your position later, you may end up on a waiting list. If that happens, I may never get the chance to do all I can to help you make money.

So let me hear from you at once! An opportunity to get paid as much as thousands of dollars a month for putting in a few minutes a day of easy enjoyable work only comes along once in a lifetime. But you have one here. I hope you take it. Please go to the next page, follow the instructions, and get started today.

CHAPTER ELEVEN

How to Get Started.

I'd like to send you all the details about my Easy Passive Income System today. The complete information package is yours for free. You'll get all the facts. Every "i" is dotted. Every "t" is crossed. You'll look everything over and decide once and for all if this is the perfect way to stay home and make money. If it is, we'll help get you signed up an Affiliate for our revolutionary health technology partner. This company is the foundation of our Easy Passive Income System. They charge a low one-time fee, which we will cover for you. Your Affiliate position will include 5,000 of your own Discount

MAKE MONEY HELPING PEOPLE

Prescription Cards. Just fill out the form on the next page and mail or fax it back to my office. I will send you complete information about our Easy Passive Income System. This information package is yours absolutely free. Then, if after looking all this over, this is the perfect way for you to make all the money you want and need, we will enroll you as an Affiliate for the health technology company who is providing the Prescription Savings Cards. And I will make sure they send your 5,000 cards directly to you. Then I will rush you my complete Easy Passive Income System. This lets lets you cash-in with all of the secrets you've discovered in this book.

"Easy Passive Income System"
FAST-AND-EASY REQUEST FORM

YES! Please tell me more! I read this book and I'm excited! Now I want to know how I can get started. So please rush me the materials that tell me how I can become a representative for the Easy Passive Income System. If accepted into this opportunity, you will help me get set up as an affiliate for the health technology company and do all you can to see to it that I get paid the largest amount of money for doing the most good for so many other people.

**RUSH ME THE COMPLETE DETAILS** that tell me how I can become a Representative for your Easy Passive Income System! I understand that there's no obligation to get all of these materials.

✔ Provide us your contact information below.

First and Last Name _____

Mailing Address _____

City/State/Zip Code _____

Mobile Phone Number _____

Email Address _____

✔ MAIL or FAX this request form to us right away.

MAIL to: Bethesda Discount Prescriptions • _Old Bethesda Hospital_
103 S. Elm St. • Goessel, KS 67053-0198

FAX to: (620) 367-2261

✔ Or use our **ONLINE SUPPORT DESK** to provide the info above to request your free Special Report:

www.GetAllTheSecrets.com/epis-info

| Invitation Code: BOOK |

Still Wondering If This is for Real? Take a Look at What a Few of Our Cardholders Had to Say:

I am senior pastor at My Liberty Church of God and Christ located in Philadelphia, PA in the West Oak Lane section of the city. I pastor about 4,000 people here at the church. The first week after I gave the Card out to my congregation, I got numerous phone calls from the members of the church that they went to the pharmacy, used their Card and had a discount on their prescription.

I was amazed. Our church was able to help our members get some discounts where they can be able to manage and budget their money and do other things.

— **Bishop Earnest E. Morris, Sr. (Philadelphia, PA)**

I filled my husband's two prescriptions at our local Hannaford store and I used my card. The first prescription's retail price was $62.99 but I only paid $13.55. The second prescription's retail price was $105.01 but I only paid $14.67 for a 90-day prescription. This was cheaper than the copay on my insurance card through my employer.

— **Sonya MacDonald (South Paris, ME)**

My wife and I befriended a gentleman approximately a year ago who had no health insurance but required medication because of a recent cranial procedure. We purchased his drugs for him at Walgreens at a cost of $297, but this time at renewal we visited our local pharmacy and saved a whopping $240! We recently found out about your organization and are informing several individuals that have no medical coverage. THANK YOU.

Bruce L. (Glassboro, NJ)

My friend is on a catastrophic plan without drug coverage and recently used this card and received a $55 discount without any hassle – super easy and he was very thankful.

— **Allison Nickel (Tacoma, WA)**

My sister-in-law Sonya gave me a card at Wal-Mart here in Columbia, SC. I had just finished shouting at the pharmacy guy telling him, "This is crazy if you think I'm going to pay $68.89 for this prescription!" So my sister-in-law told me to use the card and I did. Wow! Is all I can say. Get this! I paid only $17.64 for my prescription!

— **Pauline Sims (Columbia, SC)**

I'm a diabetic and I have to take diabetic medicine on a regular basis. Through the regular insurance company, I was paying close to $140 for my prescription medicine – four different medications. With the Card, now my medication costs me $50.

— **Nelson Geralds (Pleasantville, NJ)**

We are a prayer group here at Hope Clinic. I plan on giving these to Hope Clinic to give to their patients who are uninsured or under insured. This is why Hope Clinic got started. So people like that could get good healthcare based on their income. They are a non-profit organization. I was blessed with one of your cards that came in the mail. My husband used it first his medicine would have cost him $35 after discount it was just $13.24. I want to share our good fortune with others.

— **Tammy Neville (Lafayette, TN)**

At least one third of our patients are uninsured. They are mostly, really hard working guys that make too much money to qualify for medicaid, but they don't make enough to buy their own insurance. We have patients that take medication that doesn't work very well over a medication that they know works, but can't afford. These cards would be given to our patients that have no insurance, and are in need of some help. This is a great program. I must say, I'm very impressed.

— **Gregory VillaBona, M.D. (Dover, DE)**

My grandson takes the antibiotic Omnicef for ear infections and they have the script filled at Wal-Mart for around $80. She used the card for the refill and it cost her $25.43! When you consider the number of prescriptions filled annually by families (not to mention seniors) the potential economic impact is amazing. We owe it to our families and friends to get the card into their hands!

— **Jerry D. Turney (Scottsdale, AZ)**

I was able to save $69.74 on just one medication. Wow what a blessing.

George Nelson (Mullica Hill, NJ)

www.ingramcontent.com/pod-product-compliance
Lightning Source LLC
Chambersburg PA
CBHW020159200326
41521CB00005BA/189